WHY EVERY CONSULTANT MUST WRITE A BOOK

"How to Use a Book as a Strategy"

RAAM ANAND

STARDOM BOOKS

www.StardomBooks.com

STARDOM BOOKS
112 Bordeaux Ct.
Coppell, TX 75019, USA

Copyright © 2025 by RAAM ANAND

All rights reserved. No part of this book may be reproduced or used in any manner without written permission of the copyright owner except for the use of quotations in a book review.

FIRST EDITION NOVEMBER 2025

STARDOM BOOKS, LLC.
112 Bordeaux Ct. Coppell, TX 75019, USA

www.stardombooks.com

Stardom Books, United States
Stardom Alliance, India

The author and publishers have made all reasonable efforts to contact copyright holders for permission and apologize for any omissions or errors in the form of credits given. Corrections may be made to future editions.

WHY EVERY CONSULTANT MUST WRITE A BOOK
"How to Use a Book as a Strategy"

RAAM ANAND

p. 151
cm. 13.5 X 21.5
Category: LAN027000 LANGUAGE ARTS & DISCIPLINES/
Publishers & Publishing Industry
BUS075000 Business & Economics : Consulting

ISBN: 978-1-957456-81-2

Dedication

To those who listen deeply, solve silently, and shape outcomes behind the scenes.
This book is dedicated to you, the consultants who transform ambiguity into clarity.
The guides who help businesses find their way forward, and the quiet experts whose knowledge deserves a louder stage.
May these pages encourage you to claim authorship, not just of insights, but of your influence.
The world is listening. It's time to put your wisdom in writing.

Acknowledgements

Writing this book has been a journey shaped by the insights, experiences, and encouragement of many.

First and foremost, I extend my gratitude to the countless consultants — seasoned professionals and emerging voices — who continue to inspire and elevate the practice of consulting. Your dedication to solving complex problems and creating meaningful change is the foundation upon which this book is built.

I would like to thank my mentors, colleagues, and clients, who have challenged my thinking, sharpened my perspective, and reminded me of the actual, profound impact of thoughtful guidance and strategic clarity.

A heartfelt thanks to the team at Stardom Books for their unwavering support, editorial expertise, and commitment to helping this vision take shape.

To my family and friends, thank you for your patience, encouragement, and belief in this project, even when the writing took over everything else.

And finally, to the readers, especially the consultants looking to grow, lead, and leave a legacy—this book is for you.

Contents

Introduction		i
1.	Elevating Your Professional Status	1
2.	Clarity is Currency	11
3.	Why You're Already Ready	33
4.	The Fear of Being Seen	47
5.	Perfection Kills Potential	61
6.	Writing the Right Book	75
7.	How & Where to Get Professional Help	91
Bonus		115
About the Author		135

Introduction

Nothing happens quite by chance. It's a question of accretion of information and experience.

—Jonas Salk

In the fast-paced and ever-evolving world of consulting, standing out from the competition is both a challenge and a necessity. Whether you are an independent consultant or part of a larger firm, clients are not just hiring your services; they are buying your expertise, your insight, and your ability to solve complex problems. In such a landscape, how do you establish lasting authority, deepen trust, and differentiate yourself in a highly competitive market?

One often overlooked but potent tool is writing a book. This book, *Why Every Consultant Must Write a Book* is written for consultants like you, practicing professionals who are already helping clients solve real-world challenges yet looking for that next leap in credibility, reach, and impact. This is not a guide for aspiring novelists or creative writers. This is a strategic roadmap for experts who want to use a book as a professional asset, one that can open doors, position you as a thought leader, and even generate new streams of income.

Writing a book is a daunting and time-consuming task, especially when you're balancing client deliverables, pitching for new business, and managing the operations of your consulting practice. However, the truth is that you already have the raw material you need.

Your experience, frameworks, case studies, client successes, and observations all can be shaped into valuable intellectual property. When packaged in the form of a well-written, insightful book, it becomes a credibility-enhancing powerhouse that works for you long after you've typed the final word.

This book will guide you through every step of the process, from identifying your book's core idea to publishing and promoting it. We'll explore how consultants across various industries have utilized books to expand their practices, attract higher-value clients, secure media coverage, gain keynote speaking opportunities, and exert greater influence in their niche. You'll also find actionable advice on how to manage your time, overcome writer's block, and ensure your book not only reflects your expertise but also delivers genuine value to your readers.

Why Writing a Book Is a Game-Changer for Consultants

Consultants are in the business of trust. Your ability to win clients, retain them, and command higher fees all depends on how effectively you convey your expertise. A well-crafted book does that—and more. It's not just a marketing asset; it's a strategic instrument that reinforces your reputation, extends your visibility, and builds lasting intellectual authority.

Here are some of the core ways a book can transform your consulting practice:

Establishing Authority and Credibility

In consulting, perception often equals value. A book immediately signals that you are not just another service provider; you are an expert, a thinker, a leader in your domain. Unlike a LinkedIn post or a conference panel, a book provides depth. It allows you to unpack your ideas, demonstrate your frameworks, and show how you solve real problems. Clients, decision-makers, and even peers tend to view published authors with greater respect. In many industries, your book becomes your business card on steroids.

It tells your story, showcases your expertise, and makes the case for why you are uniquely qualified to help. When potential clients receive your book, they don't see a pitch; they see proof.

Creating Networking and Partnership Opportunities

Authors often discover that their book opens new doors, some they never imagined. Once you become a published consultant, invitations to speak at conferences, join expert panels, guest on podcasts, or collaborate with other professionals often follow. A book naturally sparks conversations. People share it, recommend it, and even use it as a reference point.

Many consultants have leveraged their books to build partnerships with larger firms, secure long-term advisory roles, or even enter new markets. Whether you're looking to build a stronger peer network, grow your client base, or collaborate with thought leaders, a book becomes a connector, a bridge between you and new opportunities.

Strengthening Your Personal Brand and Marketing Strategy

We live in the era of content. And while blogs, social media, and webinars are essential, they often compete in a noisy, short-attention world. A book offers depth and staying power. It anchors your brand, allowing you to build a consistent narrative around your consulting philosophy, methodologies, and case studies.

A book can fuel your entire marketing ecosystem. Excerpts become blog posts. Chapters become the basis for webinars or masterclasses. The core theme of your book can shape your LinkedIn strategy or email campaigns. Media outlets are more likely to feature consultants who've written books, and journalists often seek quotes from published authors over equally qualified peers without published work.

Your book becomes the backbone of your authority-driven marketing strategy—and it keeps working long after the initial launch.

Achieving Personal and Professional Fulfillment

Beyond the business impact, writing a book is a personally transformative experience. It requires you to reflect on your journey, organize your thoughts, and articulate your value in a way that's both authentic and compelling. Many consultants report that the writing process helps them clarify their methodology, sharpen their communication, and reconnect with the purpose behind their work.

There is also pride in creation. You've spent years developing your expertise—why not preserve and share it? Your book can become a legacy piece. It documents your thoughts, work, and stories. It can inspire junior consultants, educate your clients, and influence your industry long after you've left the room.

Driving Strategic Business Growth

The most overlooked aspect of publishing a book is its direct impact on your bottom line. A book can generate leads, qualify your audience, and help you move upmarket. Clients who read your book are already aligned with your approach by the time they reach out to you. That shortens the sales cycle and often increases deal size.

Books can also unlock new revenue streams. Many consultants use their books as the foundation for workshops, online courses, group programs, or corporate training packages. Some even get paid speaking opportunities or consulting retainers that originated because someone, somewhere, read their book and felt a connection.

In other words, your book can make money directly (through sales and spin-off products) and indirectly (by boosting your consulting business).

You Already Have What It Takes

If you've ever helped a client solve a complex problem, coached a team through a transition, or developed a new framework, you have something worth sharing. The idea of writing a book might feel overwhelming, but you don't have to do it all at once.

Like any consulting project, it's about breaking things down into a straightforward process, managing scope, and delivering value.

This book will be your guide. We'll cover everything from identifying the right topic to structuring your content and choosing between publishing options, as well as building a launch plan that aligns with your business goals. You'll also hear from other consultants who have written books and how the experience has transformed their careers. Ultimately, this isn't just about writing a book. It's about unlocking new levels of visibility, credibility, income, and impact. And, in a competitive, credibility-driven industry like consulting, that can make all the difference.

Let's begin!

1

Elevating Your Professional Status

"If there's a book that you want to read, but it hasn't been written yet, then you must write it."

―― **Toni Morrison**

Every generation of professionals faces a defining question, one that quietly determines who rises above the crowd and who fades into the background. For consultants, that question is not, "How much do you know?" or even, "How hard do you work?" It is this: "Why should anyone listen to you?" This is the age of expertise inflation, where every other person claims to be a strategist, a mentor, or an advisor. LinkedIn is flooded with endorsements. Podcasts are overflowing with "success stories." And social media is a constant parade of people trying to brand themselves as the next big voice in their industry. In such a crowded world, your degrees, your work experience, and your certifications, while important, are no longer enough to command attention. People no longer buy services; they buy trust. They no longer seek information; they seek insight. And trust, as every great leader and every timeless brand knows, is not given to the loudest person in the room. It's given to the person who speaks with clarity, depth, and courage, the one who has distilled their experiences into something lasting, something that outlives trends and leaves a lasting mark on their field.

The 2018 study by Edelman and LinkedIn on 'B2B Thought Leadership Impact' surveyed more than 12,000 business decision-makers across various industries.

A prominent finding indicated that 63% of decision-makers stated that *thought leadership content is a more trustworthy basis for assessing a professional's capabilities than marketing materials.* However, *only 17% believed most thought leadership content was good enough to be truly impactful.* In other words, there is a massive gap between professionals who claim expertise and those perceived as real authorities. The gap reflects both a challenge and an opportunity. If you are a consultant, specifically in customer service or business advisory, the landscape is more competitive than ever. Each individual claims to be an expert. Everyone has a LinkedIn profile, a blog, and a certification. So, how does one stand out in a market flooded with voices? How do you move from being seen as "a consultant" to being seen as *the* consultant?

One asset that metamorphoses perception faster and more credibly than any social media campaign, any seminar series, or even years of slow-earned word of mouth is a published book. It is not an eBook hidden behind a pop-up form on your website, nor a ghostwritten PDF sent to email subscribers. This refers to a professionally structured, published book with your name on the cover, sitting on Amazon, on Kindle, in someone's library, or in the hands of your potential clients. You might wonder: Why does a book matter so much in today's fast-paced digital world? It is more inclined towards what a book symbolizes. In a world obsessed with speed and convenience, writing a book signals something entirely different; it signals depth. It portrays that you have not only acquired expertise but also taken the time and care to codify it into something others can use and benefit from.

Here's the psychological truth most consultants don't fully appreciate: people equate authorship with authority. The root word for "authority" is quite literally "author". To author a book is to be seen as the originator of ideas.

It places you not just in the dominion of practitioners but in the company of thinkers and teachers. This is a powerful differentiator.

Dorie Clark's journey is a testament to how writing a book can elevate a consultant's authority and transform their career. A marketing strategist and consultant who was once a journalist first struggled to stand out from the crowd and become a prominent figure in her industry. In a competitive market, she frequently went unnoticed despite her extensive experience and strong client outcomes.

That changed in 2013 when she published her first book, Reinventing You: *Define Your Brand, Imagine Your Future*. It was not a mass-market bestseller; it achieved something far more valuable - it positioned her as a thought leader in the areas of personal branding and professional reinvention. The book opened new doors almost immediately. She was invited to contribute regularly to prestigious platforms, such as the *Harvard Business Review and Forbes,* began speaking at global forums, including the World Economic Forum, and saw a sharp rise in her consulting fees.

Major clients, including Google, Yale University, and the World Bank, began to seek her expertise. Over time, Dorie authored several more books, including *Stand Out, Entrepreneurial You,* and *The Long Game,* each reinforcing her authority and expanding her influence. Her story is a powerful testament to how publishing a book can become a turning point- a credibility marker that tells the world you are not just in the game; you are leading it.

Consultants often confuse "visibility" with "authority." You can have 10,000 followers on LinkedIn and still not be seen as a serious expert in your field. You can post content daily and still be perceived as a content creator, not a consultant. Authorship? That puts you in a league where you are assumed to have substance.

A 2021 study by Rain Group found that 82% of buyers feel more positively about a vendor after consuming their educational content. Nothing educates like a well-written book.

Therefore, the first chapter of this book starts not with tactics, not with structure, but with status.

Writing a book is not merely about publishing words; it's about repositioning yourself in the minds of your clients and peers. If you are looking to command higher fees, earn unsolicited referrals, or secure more media and speaking opportunities, then what you need is not just more exposure; it's an elevated perception. This is precisely what authorship delivers. Of course, writing a book isn't easy. It requires effort, planning, and the willingness to step into the uneasy zone of expressing your ideas with permanence. However, the returns are exponential, not only in revenue and recognition but also in personal growth and professional satisfaction.

If you still are skeptical, think about the last time you were introduced to someone as an author. Did your perception of their credibility go up or down? Did you immediately assume that they must know what they are talking about? Did they seem more serious?

This is the unspoken social contract a book creates. It invites trust, commands respect, and signals a level of mastery that few other assets can replicate. You don't have to be a celebrity consultant. You don't need a decade of experience or a massive following. What you need is a clear message, a structured approach, and the right strategy to turn your knowledge into a book that positions you as an authority in your niche.

Establishing Authority

Once your name appears on the spine of a published book, the perception of who you are and what you represent shifts almost immediately. This means you are no longer just a consultant offering services; you become someone who has ideas worth preserving, referencing, and teaching. The transformation isn't just symbolic; it's deeply psychological.

A book is a credential, not just ink on paper. In the field of consulting, especially in customer service or client experience, this kind of authority is a rare and invaluable asset.

There is no shortage of people calling themselves consultants. The market is saturated with professionals offering frameworks, empathy maps, metrics, and transformation tools.

But in a sea of noise, only a few voices rise above.

The difference isn't always knowledge; it's positioning. Authorship leads you to the top of that hierarchy.

Let's consider the story of Shep Hyken, one of the most recognized voices in customer service and experience today. Shep's career started in much the same way many consultants start, facilitating workshops, speaking at company off-sites, and running customer service training programs. However, despite years of experience, he was one among many.

The actual shift was when he published his first book, *Moments of Magic*. The book outlined Shep's approach to customer delight and set him apart from those merely offering tips and techniques. It gave his work permanence and weight.

Over time, he authored several more books: *The Cult of the Customer, The Amazement Revolution,* and *Be Amazing or Go Home*—each one reinforcing his unique perspective and expertise.

His books earned him invitations to keynote major conferences, consult with Fortune 500 companies, and appear in leading business publications. He wasn't just in the industry anymore; he was defining it.

A book provides more than visibility; it offers voice. It's not a fleeting one dependent on algorithms or ad spending, but a durable voice that carries weight in rooms you have never been in.

This change is not only reflected in public perception, but it also influences behavior. When clients see you as the author of a definitive book in your niche, they enter the relationship already respecting your expertise.

You do not have to sell yourself in the traditional sense.

There is no need for aggressive persuasion or elaborate demonstrations of value. The book has already done the heavy lifting. You are no longer being evaluated as a service provider; you are being sought after as a strategic partner.

The consulting fees you command begin to change. Studies in professional services have long shown that perceived expertise often trumps actual service delivery when it comes to pricing. In simpler terms, clients don't just pay for your time—they pay for your authority. A book allows you to charge more, not because you have changed your offering, but because you have changed how people value it.

Let's pause here and unpack why this shift happens. People equate writing a book with possessing deep, structured, and actionable knowledge. This is mainly because writing a book is a difficult task. It requires clarity of thought, a well-defined philosophy, and the ability to convey complex ideas in accessible language. It is, by design, a proof-of-work.

When someone sees that you have done this hard work, they infer that you must know your subject deeply. This is where a subtle yet powerful social dynamic comes into play: authorship being perceived as a form of leadership. While writing a book, you aren't just documenting ideas; you are shaping a narrative.

In customer service consulting, where clients often struggle to differentiate between vendors, this is a beneficial advantage. Your book becomes a filter. It helps potential clients self-identify as the right fit for your approach, saving time and energy on both sides. It also weeds out low-value engagements. You are no longer chasing work; your work starts attracting the right kind of attention.

There's also what I like to call the "authority flywheel." Once you publish a book, you are more likely to be invited to speak at events, be interviewed by media outlets, collaborate with brands, and write for high-credibility publications. Each of these opportunities, in turn, reinforces your authority.

And with each new platform, your influence compounds. You are no longer just known- you are trusted.

Suppose you have ever felt frustrated by being overlooked in client pitches despite having solid credentials. In that case, it's probably because you were missing this one asset: an authored proof of your thought leadership.

A book will not just market your services; it will memorialize your expertise.

Writing a book transforms you internally. The process demands that you clarify your thinking, organize your intellectual property, and articulate your methodology. You move away from vague expertise and develop a precise, repeatable, and teachable framework. The clarity changes how you deliver your services. It sharpens your work, makes your presentations more persuasive, and enhances your relationships with clients.

One would also discover that writing forces you to take ownership of your beliefs. Your name, published, is your stamp on the field.

Building Credibility

Authority and credibility are often used interchangeably; however, they serve distinct functions in the professional world. Authority gives you attention, but credibility earns you trust. Where authority gets you a seat at the table, credibility keeps you there.

A book acts as a form of intellectual due diligence. Jeanne Bliss, a former Chief Customer Officer at Microsoft and Land's End, went on to found CustomerBliss and consult some of the world's most admired companies. Her book, *Chief Customer Officer*, became a staple in executive boardrooms and MBA classrooms alike.

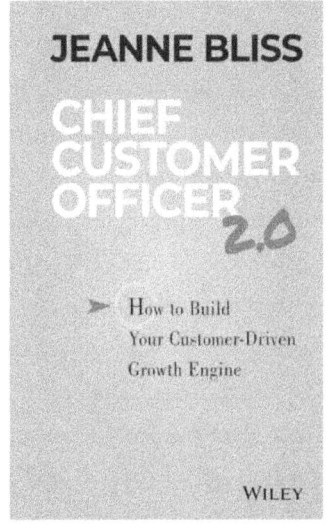

It turned out to be a sign of confidence rather than just a playbook. Her willingness to freely express her opinions, which went beyond speaking engagements and consulting reports, improved her reputation.

Over time, her reputation grew, and she became more than just a business consultant. She was now one of the voices shaping the customer experience sector. Thought leaders with published books are quoted or referenced in white papers, podcasts, and panel discussions. That halo of credibility is hard to replicate with any other asset.

Let's not forget to consider internal stakeholders. Often, the people you work with inside a client's organization—mid-level managers, department heads, and team leads—are the ones responsible for implementing your recommendations. If they don't trust your perspective, your strategies won't stick. A book also gives you built-in legitimacy with these audiences. It lends authority by proxy, making it easier for internal teams to buy into your vision.

Your book is a silent advocate, working on your behalf in rooms you are not even in. It tells potential clients, collaborators, and even competitors that you have not only shown up but also prepared. In an industry saturated with professionals claiming expertise, the most powerful differentiator isn't louder marketing or clever branding—it's clarity. Not just clarity of service but of thought, belief, and methodology. A book delivers clarity in its highest form.

By now, you have seen how authorship repositions you- from one consultant among many to a trusted go-to expert. A book isn't just a tool to gain attention; it's an anchor for credibility, a long-form testament to your seriousness, and a gateway to being taken more seriously in the rooms that matter. It turns the invisible value you bring into something tangible. If you have ever felt the frustration of being good at what you do but not being seen, of doing the work but still competing on price, of having ideas but no clear platform for them- this chapter should serve as your turning point. The perception gap you are struggling with is not a matter of skill. It's a matter of signal. And the signal that separates those who are consulted occasionally from those who are sought out consistently is authorship.

In the following chapters, we will explore how a book opens doors, builds relationships, attracts ideal clients, and creates a lasting impact. The people we call experts tomorrow will be the ones who publish their ideas today.

Key Takeaways:

- **Authority is Earned, Not Claimed:** In a crowded market where everyone is a "consultant," a published book positions you as a true authority; someone whose ideas shape the industry, not just serve it.

- **A Book Builds Instant Trust:** Clients and peers view authors as credible thought leaders. A book signals depth, commitment, and structured expertise; qualities buyers trust far more than social media content or certifications.

- **Visibility Alone Isn't Enough:** Followers and blog posts may make you visible, but authorship makes you respected. Writing a book moves you from the noise of content creators to the trusted circle of industry leaders.

- **Books Are Long-Term Assets:** Unlike social posts or webinars, a book creates lasting influence. It works for you when you're not in the room, building your brand, attracting ideal clients, and opening new opportunities.

- **The Market Rewards Clarity:** In an overcrowded consulting space, those who clearly articulate their approach, and publish it, stand out. A book is the clearest, most powerful articulation of your expertise.

***

2
CLARITY IS CURRENCY

"Too many of us are not living our dreams because we are living our fears."
———**Les Brown**

Resourcefulness is not an occasional advantage; it is your lifeblood. Every single day, you solve problems others find too messy to touch. Resilience is your armor. You juggle competing stakeholder agendas, decipher complex client environments, and deliver solutions on tight timelines. You thrive in chaos because that's where your expertise shines brightest.

Yet, despite your competence in high-pressure environments, there is one task that seems to loom larger and more intimidating than any boardroom battle: writing a book. This may sound contradictory. After all, consultants like you are no strangers to articulating ideas. You draft strategy documents, write white papers, create presentations, and communicate vision in high-stakes meetings. But somehow, when the task is to distill your thought leadership into a manuscript, hesitation creeps in. Suddenly, the clarity you bring to client problems feels clouded by self-doubt.

The drive that fuels your client engagements sputters when faced with the blank page.

Let's be clear: this resistance doesn't stem from a lack of intelligence, capability, or insight. On the contrary, your career is a testament to your intellectual horsepower and strategic discipline.

The challenge, instead, comes from a quieter, more subtle adversary: your inner narrative.

Most consultants don't need to be convinced about why writing a book makes sense. The business case is obvious.

- A book amplifies your brand and positions you as a domain authority.

- It gives your consulting practice a sharp differentiator in a saturated market.

- It opens doors to keynote speaking gigs, panel invitations, media features, and industry partnerships.

- It acts as a lasting intellectual asset; your ideas in print, creating impact long after the client engagement ends.

It's your most powerful business card. A calling card that doesn't get lost in a wallet but stays on desks, bookshelves, and in conversations. So, if the strategic logic is clear, what's holding you back?

The truth is, the most significant obstacles are not found in your calendar, your workload, or even your writing ability. The most stubborn barriers are psychological. You're not alone in facing them. These mental roadblocks are remarkably common among high-achieving professionals, especially those in consulting, where excellence is the standard and mistakes are perceived as costly.

Let's look at three of the most pervasive mindset challenges.

Perhaps you've found yourself thinking:

- "What do I have to say that hasn't already been said?"

- "There are consultants far more experienced than me. Who would want to read my perspective?"

- "I'm still figuring things out myself. Am I really the right person to write this book?"

Sound familiar? This is the voice of impostor syndrome; a persistent, nagging doubt that your achievements are somehow insufficient, or that you're not qualified enough to share your insights. But let's reframe this. You advise clients every day. You charge significant fees for your counsel. Organizations seek you out to solve problems they can't solve themselves. If your expertise didn't matter, you wouldn't be in business.

Your book is not meant to be the final word on your subject. It's meant to be your account—a reflection of your unique experiences, frameworks, and lessons learned. No one else has your combination of client stories, insights, failures, and wins. That distinct perspective is what makes your voice valuable.

Consultants are trained to produce polished work. Client deliverables are expected to be airtight—clear, actionable, and error-free. However, this mindset, while essential in client work, can be paralyzing when applied to creative endeavors, such as writing a book.

The draft of your book is not a final report. It's the start of a conversation, not the conclusion of an engagement. Waiting until every sentence is perfect is a guaranteed way never to finish. Instead, approach your book the way you approach a new consulting framework:

Start with a hypothesis. → *Test your ideas through writing.* → *Refine and improve through iterations.*

Professional writers don't produce brilliance in their first draft. They embrace messy beginnings, trusting the revision process to shape their work into something impactful. Your book deserves the same approach.

Time anxiety is perhaps the most common excuse—and the most understandable. Consultants' calendars are notoriously packed. Between billable hours, business development, team management, and personal responsibilities, finding space to write seems impossible.

But here's the truth: you will never "find" time. You will have to make it. Think of your book as a strategic initiative, not a side hobby. You don't wait for free time to craft a client proposal; you make it a priority.

Similarly, carve out intentional writing blocks, however small, and protect them like you would an important meeting.

Even one focused hour a week compounds into meaningful progress over time. Consistency, not marathon writing sessions, is what gets books written. The good news is that impostor syndrome, perfectionism, and time anxiety are not permanent features of your personality.

They are internal scripts; narratives your mind plays on repeat, often without question. And like any script, they can be rewritten.

You've helped clients transform limiting beliefs within their organizations. Now it's time to apply that same change management approach to your mindset.

Let's shift from theory to practice. Here are actionable mindset strategies designed for consultants like you—professionals who lead with logic, strategy, and a desire for tangible outcomes. Instead of seeing your book as a personal branding project (which can feel self-promotional), reframe it as an act of service to your clients and industry peers.

Ask yourself:

- What questions do my clients ask me repeatedly?

- What frameworks have helped them unlock results?

- What mistakes could they avoid if they had access to my experiences?

Your book is your way of serving those beyond your immediate client roster. It's leadership at scale. Break your book-writing journey into stages, much like a consulting engagement:

- Discovery Phase: Outline your ideas, themes, and audience pain points.

- Solution Design: Develop your chapters and key frameworks.

- Execution: Write messy first drafts without worrying about polish.

- Iteration: Refine based on feedback from editors, peers, or beta readers.

- Delivery: Publish and promote your book with the same strategic intent as you would a thought leadership white paper.

Seen this way, writing a book is not an abstract creative struggle. It's a project—one you are more than qualified to lead.

One of the most liberating truths about writing is that progress trumps perfection. A half-written manuscript is infinitely more valuable than a perfect book that lives only in your head.

Set micro-goals:

- Write 500 words a day, or 2,000 words a week.

- Finish a rough draft of each chapter before fine-tuning the prose.

- Celebrate milestones like completing your outline, your first chapter, or your first draft.

Momentum creates motivation. The more you write, the more clarity you gain.

Treat your writing sessions with the same respect you give to your billable hours—block time on your calendar. Set boundaries. Turn off notifications. Honor your creative work as essential, not optional.

If needed, build external accountability:

- Work with a writing coach or editor.

- Join a writing mastermind group.

- Publicly announce your book project to create positive peer pressure.

Your consulting career has already taught you how to analyze complexity, communicate clearly, and lead conversations that drive action. Writing a book is an extension of these skills. It is simply a new format for your leadership.

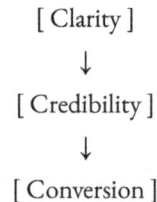

Understanding the Mental Blocks Consultants Face
Imposter Syndrome: "Why Would Anyone Read What I Have to Say?"

One of the most common inner voices that consultants face when contemplating a book is the subtle whisper of inadequacy. It doesn't yell, but it's persistent: *"Have I really done enough to write a book?"* or *"Who am I to share advice with others?"* This is classic imposter syndrome—an internal belief that your expertise is not "legitimate enough" to deserve an audience.

This doubt is particularly ironic in consulting, a profession built on insight, problem-solving, and strategic thinking. You spend your days advising leaders, guiding teams through change, and delivering tangible value. But when it comes to writing a book, the mind suddenly raises the bar to unreachable heights.

Here's what's crucial to remember: your experiences are not only valid—they are incredibly valuable.

You do not need to have advised Fortune 500 companies or spoken on global stages to write a book worth reading. The most powerful ideas often come from everyday consulting experiences: helping a mid-sized business pivot during a crisis, improving workflows that save your client hundreds of hours, managing complex stakeholder dynamics—these are gold mines of wisdom. When you share these real-world scenarios, they build trust. They offer relatability. And most importantly, they help others grow.

Rather than asking "Am I qualified to write this book?", reframe the question to "Who could benefit from the lessons I've already learned the hard way?"

Shift from Self-Doubt to Service

A powerful antidote to imposter syndrome is shifting the focus away from yourself and toward the people you're writing for. Think about the aspiring consultants who haven't yet faced the kind of client tension you have, or the business leaders struggling to implement the exact kind of change you've guided others through. When you write with the intention to serve, the fear of not being "enough" starts to fade.

The truth is, readers aren't looking for perfection or prestige. They're looking for resonance. And nothing resonates more than lived experience shared with honesty and generosity.

Perfectionism: The Silent Killer of Consultant Authorship

If you've spent years in the consulting world, you know that excellence is the currency of your profession. You are rewarded for precision, praised for clarity, and respected for your ability to distill complexity into actionable insights. A single misplaced decimal in a financial model or an unclear recommendation in a slide deck could mean the difference between client trust and scrutiny. Over time, this pursuit of flawlessness becomes second nature. It's not merely a professional standard; it's how you define your competence.

So when the idea of writing a book enters your world—a book that will carry your name, your voice, and your ideas out into the world—it's no surprise that perfectionism follows closely behind. The same perfectionism that sharpens your PowerPoint decks and polishes your strategy reports now shadows your every sentence. Only this time, it doesn't help you move forward. It holds you back.

In the consulting arena, perfectionism is often viewed as a strength. It ensures that every deliverable is client-ready, every recommendation is defensible, and every piece of analysis is watertight. But in the world of book writing, that same perfectionism becomes a form of creative paralysis. It whispers in your ear that your first draft must read like the final chapter of a bestselling author.

It convinces you that your outline must be flawless before you write the first sentence. It makes you believe that unless you achieve brilliance in your first attempt, it's not worth continuing.

And so, you sit with your laptop open, cursor blinking on a blank page, tweaking the first paragraph over and over. You write a sentence and then delete it, doubting its clarity, its insight, its value. Chapter one consumes your attention, and you tell yourself you'll start chapter two once you're sure the first one is perfect. But it never feels quite right. The structure feels wobbly. The voice feels uncertain. The flow feels off. Instead of progressing to the next chapter, you find yourself stuck, endlessly polishing a fragment of your book that only you have seen. The result is predictable and painful: your book remains trapped in your mind. What could have been a powerful tool for your career, a platform for your thought leadership, a legacy for your ideas, stays unwritten, gathering dust in the corners of your ambition.

But there is another way to think about this process, one that breaks the chains of perfectionism and frees your creativity: books are meant to be messy at first. Think about how you approach your consulting work. When you're developing a new framework for a client, do you expect it to be perfect from the start? Of course not. You begin with hypotheses, rough drafts of models, and preliminary research, and then refine them through client conversations, internal brainstorming, and iterative analysis. Your frameworks evolve. They don't arrive fully formed; they are sculpted through use and feedback. Your book is no different.

The first draft of your manuscript is not the final strategy deck you'll present to the world. It's the scaffolding. It's the wireframe of your ideas. It's the messy whiteboard session where you pour out thoughts, stories, frameworks, and lessons, knowing full well that they will be refined later. This messiness is not a sign of failure. It's evidence that you're doing the hard work of creation.

Even the most celebrated authors in the world—those who have written books that sit on bestseller lists for years—do not write clean, polished manuscripts on the first try.

They write messy, fragmented, awkward first drafts. They wrestle with self-doubt, cut entire chapters, and rewrite passages multiple times. There is a reason books go through multiple drafts, editing rounds, and, later, updated editions. Writing is an iterative process. Clarity does not precede writing; it emerges from it.

Because you're an expert in your domain, your first draft should reflect that expertise perfectly. But writing a book is not the same as delivering a client workshop or presenting a strategy review. In those contexts, you are sharing conclusions. In your book, you are exploring ideas. You're translating years of consulting experience, client stories, and hard-won lessons into a format that other people—people outside your immediate professional circle—can understand, apply, and find meaning in. That takes time. And yes, it takes rewriting.

It is helpful to view your book not as a finished structure from day one but as a construction project that evolves. Imagine starting with scaffolding. At first, it wasn't lovely. It's incomplete. Wires are exposed. Beams are unpainted. But without that scaffolding, the building would collapse. Similarly, your first draft will have gaps. It may lack polish. The flow might feel clunky. But those rough edges are what allow you to refine, restructure, and ultimately create something enduring.

The challenge for consultants might be that this creative process feels uncomfortable. In your professional world, messiness is something to be cleaned up before the client ever sees it. But when you're writing a book, you are both the creator and the editor. There's no client to impress in draft one.

The only person watching is you. And sometimes, you are your harshest critic.

One of the greatest myths about writing is that inspiration strikes fully formed. The reality is far less glamorous. Most of the writing process happens in the trenches: writing when you're tired, writing when you're unsure, writing when the words feel clunky. But the act of writing itself creates clarity. The more you write, the more you understand your message.

Another common misconception is that the book must reflect your complete expertise from day one. But your book is not an encyclopedia. It is a curated selection of your insights, tailored for the audience you want to reach. You are not obligated to cover everything you know. You are simply offering a perspective that can help, inspire, or guide your readers. And perspectives, by nature, evolve. The book you write today reflects who you are today. If your ideas shift in the future, there is always room for another edition, another book, or another platform to share those evolutions.

So, what do you do from here?

You start. You let go of the polished, perfect image you have in your mind and instead focus on making progress. Write your first messy chapter. Then your second. Keep going, knowing that you will reevaluate and refine your approach. Trust the process. Trust your professional rigor to catch what needs fixing in later drafts. But for now, write.

Perfectionism will still knock at your door. That's okay. Acknowledge it, thank it for trying to protect your standards, and then move forward anyway. The first draft is not where your legacy is defined; it's where your ideas take shape. And someday soon, when you hold your finished book in your hands, you'll be grateful you allowed yourself to begin imperfectly.

Embracing Progress Over Perfection

When you've spent years in consulting, you learn to operate in a world where excellence is expected and results matter. Deadlines aren't optional. Deliverables aren't vague. Every project, whether it's a market-entry strategy or an operational turnaround, follows a structured process. There's a beginning, a middle, and an end, punctuated by milestones, check-ins, and client feedback. You are accustomed to working in iterations—first, a draft framework, then a refined model, followed by a polished final presentation.

And yet, when you sit down to write a book, all that process seems to evaporate. You find yourself staring at a blank page, waiting for some mythical wave of inspiration to strike.

You delay writing because the ideas don't feel perfect yet. You tell yourself that next weekend, when things are calmer, or after the next big project wraps up, you'll finally sit down and write. But next weekend never comes, and your ideas remain trapped in your mind.

This is where one of the most liberating shifts occurs, not only in your writing process but also in your mindset as a consultant stepping into authorship. It's the shift from chasing magnificence to embracing momentum.

Momentum over magnificence. Movement over mastery.

Writing a book is a professional commitment. Inspiration may come and go, but consistency creates results.

Slowly but surely, your chapters take shape. Your ideas become clearer. Your confidence as a writer grows. This approach is less glamorous than the Hollywood image of an author locking themselves in a cabin and emerging with a completed manuscript. But it's far more realistic—and sustainable—for someone balancing a demanding consulting career. Of course, consistency doesn't happen automatically. In the client world, your accountability is built in. You have deadlines, project plans, and stakeholder expectations driving your actions. With your book, those external pressures don't exist; unless you create them.

Writing also has a way of clarifying your thinking. You may start with an idea you believe is crystal clear, only to discover gaps as you try to explain it on the page. That's not a flaw in your expertise—it's the nature of translating ideas from spoken frameworks and slide decks into narrative form. The act of writing reveals what you truly know and what needs further reflection.

When you commit to writing consistently, you reconnect with your ideas in a way that deepens your understanding of them. Your frameworks, methodologies, and philosophies sharpen as you write them down. Your thought leadership matures, not only because you've articulated it, but because the act of articulation forces you to confront and refine your assumptions.

And that's where growth happens.

In your consulting practice, you value feedback. You refine your strategies based on client input and market realities. Why should writing your book be any different? Your first draft is your working hypothesis. Subsequent drafts are your refined solution. By the time your book reaches readers, it will have benefited from multiple rounds of iteration, just like your best client solutions do.

One day, you'll look back and marvel at the manuscript you've built. Not because every writing session was inspired, but because you showed up consistently, trusting that progress compounds over time. And it does.

This iterative writing process mirrors your journey as a consultant. You didn't become an expert overnight. You built your expertise project by project, client by client, mistake by mistake. Writing your book is an extension of that journey—a chance to reflect on what you've learned, distill your insights, and share them with a broader audience. And when the book is finally complete, when your manuscript is polished and ready for publication, the satisfaction will be immense. Not because the process was easy, but because you navigated it with the same determination and discipline that has fueled your consulting success.

Your consulting career has prepared you for this. You already have the tools: strategic thinking, structured problem-solving, and a commitment to excellence. Now, it's simply a matter of applying those tools to a new challenge.

You've solved complex business problems. You've advised leadership teams through uncertainty.

You've helped organizations pivot, grow, and thrive. Writing a book is another project—different in form, but similar in spirit.

So, schedule the writing sessions. Set the deadlines. Find your accountability partners. And begin.

Not tomorrow. Not next weekend. Today. Because your book won't write itself, but with momentum on your side, magnificence will follow.

You Already Have What It Takes

If you've ever led a team through uncertainty, developed a new methodology, or solved a problem no one else saw coming, you've already done something more complex than writing a book. The challenge is not whether you're capable. The challenge is quieting the doubts, silencing the perfectionist, and creating a system that lets you write with discipline, purpose, and confidence.

The internal resistance may not disappear completely. But with awareness and structure, it becomes manageable. And once you break through that resistance, what emerges isn't just a manuscript, it's a deeper understanding of your own voice, your own value, and your own vision.

That, perhaps, is the most powerful return on investment any consultant could ask for.

Breaking the Myth of Perfection: Writing with Confidence, Not Caution

In the consulting world, perfectionism is often mistaken for excellence. It's worn like a badge of honor, cultivated over years of crafting strategy decks where each slide is carefully curated, where a misplaced decimal point or a poorly worded insight could erode trust in the room. Consultants learn early on that precision is currency. It wins clients, earns confidence, and secures results. You are trained to leave nothing to chance. The expectations of your clients demand it. When you advise leaders making billion-dollar decisions, there is no room for sloppy thinking.

In this world, perfectionism isn't vanity—it's a form of professional responsibility. Your attention to detail, your insistence on clarity, your endless revising of frameworks until they are watertight—these habits are not weaknesses. They are survival skills.

And yet, when you sit down to write a book, these same habits that once fueled your success begin to work against you. Where once perfectionism drove better client outcomes, now it becomes the voice that whispers, "Don't start until you know exactly what to say."

It's the voice that says, "This paragraph isn't ready," or "Your argument isn't sharp enough yet." Slowly, without realizing it, you find yourself stuck. Not because you lack ideas. Not because you lack expertise. But the very mindset that made you a successful consultant is now keeping you from becoming an author.

Perfectionism doesn't simply slow you down in the writing process. Left unchecked, it paralyzes you. It stops you from even beginning. Because if the first draft can't be flawless, why bother writing it at all?

Your book deserves the same process-driven mindset. You are not creating a final product in your first draft. You are building a framework of ideas, testing how they hold together, refining them as you write. Some chapters will flow easily; others will feel clunky and uncertain. Some ideas will feel sharp and clear from the start; others will require multiple rewrites before they resonate. But all of this is part of the journey. The trap of perfectionism is that it confuses the *result* with the *process*. You know what a great book should sound like because you've read many. You admire the clarity of Jim Collins, the pragmatism of Clayton Christensen, and the storytelling of Simon Sinek. But what you don't see are the drafts behind the scenes—the sentences they deleted, the chapters they rewrote, the days they stared at the screen struggling to find the right words.

No great business book starts great. It became great through revision. And the sooner you allow yourself the freedom to write badly at first, the sooner you will find your authentic voice. This process is humbling, especially for consultants who are used to controlling every variable.

In your client work, you mitigate risks, anticipate objections, and create plans designed to avoid failure. But in writing, failure—in the form of imperfect drafts, clunky sentences, and unclear arguments—is part of the creative process. It's how you learn what your message is.

You may find this uncomfortable at first. Sitting with an incomplete chapter feels vulnerable. Admitting that you don't yet have the perfect opening sentence feels like weakness. But what if you reframed this discomfort? What if, instead of seeing imperfection as a flaw, you saw it as evidence of progress?

Every rough draft is proof that you've started. Every awkward chapter is a stepping stone to clarity. The only people who never write bad drafts are the ones who never write at all. Your career has prepared you for this kind of work more than you think. After all, you've led teams through uncertain market environments. You've made recommendations based on incomplete data, trusting your analytical instincts to fill in the gaps. You've presented draft strategies to skeptical stakeholders, knowing that their feedback would strengthen your solution. Your book asks for the same courage.

Instead of waiting for inspiration, treat your manuscript like a strategic initiative. Break it down into manageable parts. Start with a rough outline, knowing it will evolve. Write the first chapter as a draft, not a final report. Get your ideas onto the page before you judge them. Then step back, reflect, and refine. Over time, your messy manuscript will begin to take shape. Clarity will emerge from consistency, not perfection.

Remember that your first draft is not for public consumption. No one will see it but you and, perhaps later, your editor. You are not presenting your ideas to a global audience in draft one. You are simply exploring your thoughts in private. There is safety in this phase of the process, a quiet space where you can think aloud without judgment.

Of course, your perfectionist tendencies will try to interfere. They will tell you that your ideas aren't ready. That your writing isn't good enough.

You need to conduct further research, read one more book, and take one additional course before you begin. These voices will seem convincing because they align with your professional standards and expectations. But they are not protecting your excellence—they are delaying your progress.

The danger is not in writing something imperfect. The danger is in never writing at all. At some point, you must begin. Not because your ideas are fully formed, but because they will never become fully formed until you start working them out on the page. Writing clarifies thinking. You'll discover what you truly believe as you write your arguments down, wrestle with counterpoints, and craft examples to illustrate your points.

You'll also begin to find your writing voice, something distinct from your client-facing communication. In consulting, your tone is measured, precise, and sometimes formal. In your book, your voice can be more human, more reflective, more conversational. This voice will evolve as you write. You may start out sounding like a white paper. Over time, you'll sound like yourself. And then, one day, almost without realizing it, you will look back and see how far you've come. Chapters that once felt incoherent will now read smoothly. Ideas that once seemed scattered will now flow logically. Your messy beginnings will have transformed into a coherent manuscript.

But none of this happens if you don't allow yourself to start getting messy.

What's worth noting is that your book will not only reflect your ideas, but also your personal growth—writing forces you to slow down and articulate what you've internalized over years of experience. It requires you to confront your assumptions, challenge your thinking, and clarify your purpose. In this way, writing your book becomes not only a professional achievement but a personal transformation.

When you let go of perfectionism, you open the door to authenticity. Instead of posturing as an all-knowing authority, you speak as a seasoned professional sharing what you've learned. Readers don't need you to be perfect. They need you to be helpful. They need your frameworks, your insights, and your lessons learned from the trenches of consulting work.

They are looking for guidance, not flawless prose.

And when your book finally reaches them—when they underline your sentences, share your ideas in team meetings, and apply your frameworks to their business challenges; they won't care whether your first draft was messy. They will only care that you dared to write it. Perfectionism will not leave you entirely. It will still whisper in your ear as you revise, urging you to polish a sentence one more time. That's okay. There is a place for excellence in the editing phase. But let drafting be messy. Let your first version be a rough prototype. Later, you can refine it with the same sharp eye you bring to your client work.

Ultimately, the goal is progress, not perfection. Books, like strategy engagements, evolve through cycles of creation and improvement. No single draft defines the whole project. What defines it is your willingness to start, your discipline to continue, and your openness to refine along the way. So if you're waiting for the perfect moment to start writing, stop waiting. It will never arrive. Life will always be busy. Your ideas will always feel incomplete. You will always feel you could be better prepared. Begin anyway.

Write the first imperfect chapter. Draft the clunky framework. Put your unpolished thoughts on the page. Trust that clarity and quality will come, not at the start, but through the process. Because in the end, your book is not a monument to perfectionism. It is a testament to your journey, your work, and your willingness to share what you've learned. And the world doesn't need a perfect book that was never written.

Letting Go of Perfectionism

Set Practical, Professional Milestones — One of the simplest and most effective shifts a consultant can make when approaching a book is to treat it like a professional engagement. You wouldn't attempt to deliver an entire digital transformation strategy to a client in a single sitting. Instead, you'd break it down into phases, discovery, development, testing, refinement, and implementation. Apply that same structured mindset to your manuscript. Create manageable milestones for your writing. Break down chapters into outlines, outlines into sections, and sections into writing sprints. Each writing session doesn't need to produce a finished chapter. It only needs to move you forward. When you approach your book as a set of iterative deliverables rather than a single, flawless masterpiece, the task becomes not just doable, but predictable and progress-driven.

Think Like a Strategist, Not a Sculptor — The myth of the "perfect first draft" is one of the most damaging ideas in the creative process. Consultants often delay writing because the words in their head feel unpolished on the page.

But no strategy you deliver to a client is born perfect; it evolves through data, feedback, and revision. Treat your manuscript the same way. Think of your first draft as your MVP, minimum viable product. Microsoft, Amazon, and Google have all grown empires by releasing imperfect versions of their products, learning from feedback, and iterating based on real-world usage. Your book is no different. What matters is momentum, not mastery.

A messy draft is a sign of action. A perfect idea that lives only in your head? That's just potential, not progress.

Overcoming Fear of Public Scrutiny

Putting Your Ideas on the Line – Writing a book takes your ideas out of the boardroom and into the world. Unlike a closed-door client workshop or a confidential executive report, a book lives in public. It can be quoted, shared, praised—and critiqued. For many consultants, this visibility triggers discomfort. The fear of being wrong, misinterpreted, or challenged can lead to hesitancy.

This fear is not irrational, it's human. You've worked hard to build a reputation for credibility and control. Publishing a book feels like opening the gates to the unpredictable. But here's the truth: vulnerability does not diminish authority. It strengthens it.

Lead with Transparency – Today's readers crave authenticity. They are not looking for a polished guru who has never made a mistake. They're looking for real people who've learned through lived experience. When you share your journey—wins and stumbles alike, you build trust.

Being honest about what didn't work, what you learned the hard way, or what surprised you in a consulting engagement adds more value than a sanitized success story. Transparency transforms your book from a monologue into a conversation—one where the reader feels seen, understood, and inspired to act.

Adopt a Growth Perspective – Critique is inevitable. But in the consulting world, feedback is a tool, not a threat. Think of public response to your book the way you treat client feedback on a proposal—it's not personal; it's constructive.

Use reviews, questions, and reader conversations to refine your message, build future editions, or create supplementary content.

Thought leadership is not about being untouchable. It's about being teachable. The most respected voices in any industry are those who evolve. Writing a book is not the final word on your expertise, it's a starting point for deeper growth and greater conversations.

Writing Within the Demands of a Consultant's Life

Mastering Time Management – One of the most common objections consultants have is simple: "I just don't have the time."

Between client meetings, travel, proposals, and emergencies, your calendar is often a battleground. But let's be honest, your most important commitments always find space. Just as you block out hours for key deliverables or client strategy sessions, you must block time for your book. It deserves that same level of seriousness.

Block Time Like a Client Meeting – Treat your writing sessions with the same respect you'd give your most valuable client. Put it on your calendar. Protect it. Show up.

Even two focused writing blocks per week can lead to a complete manuscript within months. The key is consistency, not quantity.

Your book doesn't need hours of uninterrupted solitude, it needs regular, dedicated attention.

Maximize Micro-Moments – Busy professionals often underestimate how much can be done in small windows of time. Use your commute to brainstorm chapter themes. Use voice notes after a meeting to capture a client insight you could turn into a case study. Use 15-minute breaks to rough out bullet points for your next section.

At Stardom Books, we've seen this modular approach, writing in bite-sized chunks, help dozens of consultants move forward without burning out. Writing doesn't require a retreat. It requires a rhythm.

The Power of Support Systems

Don't Write Alone — Consultants are collaborative by nature. You solve problems in teams, ideate with clients, and refine ideas through discussion. Writing a book should be no different. Find or create a circle of fellow consultant-authors. Join a writers' group that meets weekly or biweekly. Share goals. Celebrate wins. Get unstuck together. At Stardom Circle, we've seen firsthand how peer accountability accelerates authorship and sustains momentum.

Leverage Professional Help — Just as your clients rely on your expertise, you can benefit from outside guidance too. A book coach can help you structure your ideas. An editor can bring polish to your words. A publishing strategist can align your book with your business goals. You don't have to do this alone, and frankly, you shouldn't.

Making the Book Serve the Business

Your Book Is Not a Detour, It's a Growth Strategy — Writing a book is not a distraction from your consulting work; it's an extension of it. Done right, it reinforces your niche, deepens your message, and draws ideal clients to you.

If you consult in a specialized space, digital transformation, sustainability, organizational culture—your book can plant a flag of authority. It becomes a pre-conversion tool that educates, engages, and excites your audience before they ever pick up the phone.

Build Your Brand Story Into Every Page — Every chapter, every anecdote, and every insight should echo the values of your consulting brand. Use the book to showcase your approach, voice, and client philosophy. The result? A powerful, portable form of marketing that doesn't feel like selling, it feels like serving.

Confidence is the Catalyst — Consulting success is built on confidence: confidence in your frameworks, your thinking, and your ability to create change. Writing a book is no different. You don't need to become someone else to be an author—you simply need to trust the expertise you already have.

Your experience is valuable. Your voice is needed. And your book is waiting.

Key Takeaways:

- **Recognize the Real Blocks:** Imposter syndrome, perfectionism, and fear of being judged aren't signs you're unqualified—they're common challenges faced by even the most seasoned consultants.

- **Momentum Over Mastery:** Don't wait for the "perfect" moment or manuscript. Make steady progress by breaking your book into manageable parts, and value movement over meticulousness.

- **Build a Support Ecosystem:** Surround yourself with like-minded consultant-authors or mentors. Accountability groups and professional editors can keep you focused, motivated, and on track.

- **See Writing as a Business Asset:** Don't treat your book as a side project—it's a strategic tool that reinforces your consulting brand, deepens your authority, and opens new doors for growth.

***

3

Why You're Already Ready

"Your network is your net worth."

———**Porter Gale**

In the world of consulting, relationships are the currency that fuels growth. Every major deal, strategic partnership, and long-term client engagement you've landed likely didn't start with a cold email or a formal pitch deck. It began with a conversation, a mutual connection, a handshake at a conference, or a casual chat over coffee. Consulting, despite its frameworks and methodologies, remains a people-driven business. Trust is built one interaction at a time.

Picture this: You're attending an industry summit, the kind where the air hums with opportunity. In breakout sessions and networking lounges, conversations spark over shared challenges and bold ideas. You find yourself face-to-face with decision-makers—CEOs, VPs, founders, and fellow consultants. Each exchange holds the potential to plant the seed of a future collaboration. Now imagine that as you introduce yourself, you don't just say, "I'm a consultant specializing in transformation strategy." Instead, you add, "I'm also the author of *Transforming with Clarity: A New Model for Change Leadership*." Then, without hesitation, you hand them a signed copy of your book. In that moment, something shifts. The conversation deepens. Their body language changes—curiosity flickers across their face, and they lean in, genuinely intrigued. They ask you about your writing process, your sources of inspiration, and your unique perspective.

What started as a simple introduction has transformed into a meaningful dialogue. By the end of the conversation, you're no longer just another consultant in the room. You're a thought leader. A published author. Someone whose ideas are worth paying attention to.

This shift isn't imaginary. It's the real-world experience of countless consultants who have embraced authorship as a strategic tool. And it can be your reality too. The beauty of a book is that it travels further than you can. Long after the conference ends, your book sits on their office shelf or their Kindle library, quietly reinforcing your authority. It may be quoted in their next leadership meeting, recommended to a peer, or gifted to another decision-maker. What began as a brief encounter becomes a lasting presence.

And here's the thing: in a world overflowing with digital noise—webinars, podcasts, and LinkedIn posts—books still carry a weight of credibility that few other mediums can match. A book requires commitment. It reflects depth of thought. It suggests that you've taken the time not only to master your craft but to articulate it in a way that others can learn from. Consider the impact of that perception. Clients who may have initially viewed you as just another consultant suddenly see you in a different light. You are no longer only someone who executes projects; you are someone who shapes perspectives. You are no longer simply solving problems; you are advancing the conversation around them.

Networking, when approached transactionally, feels superficial. But when your book becomes the centerpiece of that connection, the dynamic changes. Instead of pitching your services, you are offering your ideas. Instead of selling yourself, you are sharing your story. And people respond to stories. They remember them.

Reflect on your own professional experiences. How many relationships deepened because someone shared a personal insight or an unexpected point of view? How often did a casual conversation lead to a client engagement simply because the other person saw something valuable in your perspective? Your book amplifies that moment exponentially.

Now, let's step outside the conference hall for a moment. Picture a client you've been nurturing for months—sending articles, offering free advice, waiting for the right time to pitch a project. One day, instead of sending another market trend report, you mail them a signed copy of your book with a handwritten note:

"Thought you might enjoy some of the frameworks we've been discussing. Chapter 4, in particular, speaks to the challenges we explored last quarter. Looking forward to hearing your thoughts." That small gesture does something no cold pitch ever could. It humanizes you. It builds trust. It positions you as a generous expert, not a vendor chasing a sale.

And what happens next? Perhaps they read the book and reach out with questions. They could share it with their leadership team and invite you to lead a strategy workshop. Or maybe they appreciate the gesture, keeping you top of mind when the next opportunity arises. In every scenario, your book opens doors. And it's not only clients who take notice. Event organizers, podcast hosts, and industry publications—they are constantly searching for voices that bring fresh perspectives to their audiences. A book makes it easier for them to find you. It becomes your calling card, your platform, your introduction to people you haven't yet met.

Imagine receiving an email one day:

"Hi, I recently read your book and loved your approach to organizational transformation. We're hosting a panel on leadership agility next month and would love to have you join us as a speaker."

That invitation wasn't a result of hours spent cold-pitching conference organizers. It came because your book found its way into the right hands. This is the network effect of authorship. One book. Countless ripple effects.

Of course, this doesn't happen by magic. It happens because your book reflects real substance. It happens because you wrote something that speaks to the challenges your clients face and the aspirations they hold. Your book doesn't need to be perfect—it needs to be useful.

Clients are not looking for literary masterpieces from consultants. They are looking for clarity, insight, and guidance. They want to know that you understand their world and that you have a framework for helping them navigate it. Your book gives them that reassurance before you ever step into their boardroom.

Some consultants hesitate at this stage. They worry that writing a book will feel self-promotional, that handing someone a copy will come across as arrogant. But think of it this way: you are not handing them a sales brochure. You are offering them value. You are giving them something they can learn from, apply, and reflect on—even if they never hire you. That is the kind of generosity that builds trust, not suspicion.

And here's what often surprises first-time authors: your book will reach people you didn't know were watching. Someone in your LinkedIn network may buy a copy, share a chapter with their team, and recommend you to a colleague. A past client may stumble across your name in an airport bookstore and remember the impact you had on their business. A future partner may come across your book in an industry blog and reach out with a collaboration idea.

These moments cannot be orchestrated in advance. But they cannot happen at all if your book doesn't exist.

Beyond the tangible connections, something else happens when you step into the role of an author. You begin to carry yourself differently. You speak with greater clarity. You show up with greater confidence. The very act of writing forces you to distill your thoughts, sharpen your frameworks, and articulate your approach in ways that resonate. Your book becomes an anchor in your professional narrative. Instead of introducing yourself as "a consultant who works on strategy and transformation," you introduce yourself as "the author of *[Your Book Title]*, where I help leaders rethink how they drive sustainable change." That subtle shift in language reframes how people perceive your role—and how you perceive yourself.

It's also worth noting that your book continues working for you long after you've written it. A strategy deck serves its purpose in a single presentation.

A client memo addresses a moment in time. But a book lives on. It reaches new audiences, sparks new conversations, and generates new opportunities, often when you least expect it. In this way, your book becomes a scalable asset. As a consultant, your time is finite. You can only be in so many meetings, lead so many workshops, and take on so many clients. But your book can reach thousands, tens of thousands, maybe more, without you being in the room.

And isn't that, in the end, the definition of leverage? To build something once and let it create value repeatedly, without your direct effort. This is why the most successful consultants treat their book not as a vanity project, but as a strategic investment. Yes, writing takes time. Yes, it will push you outside your comfort zone. But the return on that investment—measured in relationships deepened, credibility enhanced, and opportunities created—is extraordinary.

So the next time you find yourself in a room full of decision-makers, ask yourself: Who do you want to be?

The consultant who shares a business card... or the consultant who hands them a book that changes how they think?

The difference between the two is not talent or expertise. It's the choice to write.

And once you make that choice, your network—and your career—will never be the same.

Networking Opportunities

For consultants, a book isn't just a publication—it's a powerful networking catalyst that can open doors even the best elevator pitch can't. When you write a book, you create a lasting piece of intellectual capital that continues to represent your expertise and value, even after the meeting is over.

A book positions you as more than a service provider—it makes you a thought leader. It naturally sparks curiosity, serves as a conversation starter, and invites deeper dialogue. Whether you're meeting a potential client, connecting with peers, or attending a conference, your book becomes an entry point for meaningful interactions.

The content of your book becomes a bridge—one that leads to long-term client relationships, strategic partnerships, and collaborations with industry leaders. It helps people understand not just *what* you do, but *how* you think—and that's often the key to building trust in consulting.

And what better way to spark those conversations than by showcasing your book on LinkedIn? Sharing insights and stories from your book positions you as a credible authority in your field. It encourages engagement from other professionals, helps you attract the right kind of attention, and can accelerate connections that would otherwise take months of outreach to establish. For consultants seeking to expand their influence and reach, authorship provides a direct line to the individuals who matter most.

Once you've authored a book, the dynamics of networking shift in your favor; there's a strong possibility that decision-makers, clients, or fellow consultants have already encountered your work through professional circles or industry discussions. Even if they haven't, simply presenting your book during an introduction immediately distinguishes you from the crowd. You're no longer just another consultant in the room—you're someone with a clearly defined point of view, someone with the confidence and clarity to publish it.

That shift in perception can open powerful doors. Suddenly, you're seen as someone worth engaging further—possibly leading to an invitation for a one-on-one meeting, a strategic partnership discussion, or even a consulting opportunity. Your book becomes more than a calling card—it becomes a symbol of trust and authority. It transforms you from a service provider into a thought partner. In the landscape of high-stakes consulting, that's a monumental advantage.

Beyond individual interactions, writing and promoting a book places you at the center of ongoing industry dialogue. Your ideas begin to circulate widely through panel discussions, podcasts, webinars, and digital platforms like LinkedIn. These touchpoints naturally attract other experts, clients, and collaborators who resonate with your insights.

Consultants thrive on trust and visibility, and a book facilitates both. It helps you forge connections that lead to joint ventures, speaking engagements, and co-authored content with respected voices in your field. Each of these opportunities enhances your visibility and reinforces your credibility, helping you stand out from the crowd and deepen your influence in the consulting world.

Case Study: Alan Weiss and Million Dollar Consulting

Alan Weiss is one of the most well-known names in the consulting world. With a background in organizational development and management consulting, he had already built a solid solo practice. However, the publication of his book *Million Dollar Consulting* in 1992 elevated his status from a successful practitioner to an industry-defining thought leader.

Before the book, Weiss was respected within certain consulting and corporate circles. However, *Million Dollar Consulting* provided him with a powerful platform to share his contrarian ideas about value-based pricing, independent consulting models, and the importance of effective positioning. The book quickly became a go-to resource for consultants seeking to scale their income and influence, and over time, it was translated into multiple languages and underwent several updated editions.

From Consultant to Industry Authority

With the book's growing popularity, Alan Weiss began receiving invitations to speak at top-tier conferences, corporate retreats, and business schools worldwide. Consulting networks, executive coaching platforms, and Fortune 500 clients began reaching out—not just because of referrals, but because they had read his work or heard of him through their professional networks.

Suddenly, he wasn't just seen as a consultant for hire—he was seen as a *mentor* to other consultants, a strategic advisor to CEOs, and a benchmark name in the field of high-fee consulting.

Networking Power Amplified

Weiss's book opened doors to high-level conversations with business leaders and aspiring consultants alike. At conferences, people would approach him not with generic questions but referencing specific passages from his book. On platforms like LinkedIn and industry forums, his book created a constant stream of inbound interest. It wasn't just about visibility—it was about visibility *with authority.*

He leveraged this momentum to launch the Million Dollar Consulting® College, a training and mentorship program for consultants, and built a global community around his work. His subsequent books and consulting products found an already engaged audience—one that was initially built through the impact of his first major publication.

Impact on Career and Influence

Today, Alan Weiss is credited with shaping the mindset of independent consultants globally. He has authored over 60 books, but *Million Dollar Consulting* became the cornerstone of his brand.

His network includes top-tier consultants, senior executives, and global business influencers—not because he cold-emailed his way in, but because his book served as the entry ticket to meaningful professional relationships.

Collaborative Ventures

Writing a book can open the door to powerful collaborations for consultants, be it co-authoring projects, research partnerships, or strategic consulting alliances. When you publish a book, you don't just showcase your knowledge—you establish yourself as a thought leader worth working with. This credibility makes you a desirable collaborator for others in your field.

The process of writing, publishing, and promoting a book naturally expands your professional network. As you engage with readers, fellow consultants, and industry leaders through book launches, webinars, conferences, or online forums, you begin to attract like-minded professionals. These interactions often evolve into joint ventures, content collaborations, or shared client engagements that amplify the visibility and impact of both parties.

Books help consultants move beyond isolated practice into collective influence. Co-authoring a book, contributing to anthologies, or developing thought leadership content in partnership with others can significantly boost your reach. It not only exposes you to your collaborator's audience but also fosters cross-pollination of ideas, which is essential in today's fast-evolving consulting landscape.

A prime example of the power of collaboration through authorship is the partnership between Patrick Lencioni, founder of "The Table Group," and various business leaders and consultants with whom he has co-authored works or whitepapers. Lencioni's books on organizational health and team dynamics have not only shaped leadership practices across industries but also led to deeper consulting engagements, speaking invitations, and long-term client partnerships, many of which began through shared thought leadership efforts.

For consultants, writing a book is not just about elevating your personal brand. It's also about inviting collaboration, sparking dialogue, and building alliances that can lead to bigger opportunities and a broader professional impact. Through these collaborative ventures, your authority strengthens, and your consulting business becomes more than a solo endeavor: it becomes a hub of influence.

Another compelling example of the power of collaboration through authorship comes from the consulting world, where co-authored books have led to significant joint ventures and expanded the influence of their authors. Take, for instance, the collaboration between consultants and business strategists who combine their domain expertise to produce high-impact resources that not only establish authority but also create new avenues for engagement.

A notable case is the partnership between Peter Block and Flawless Consulting, which started with the publication of *Flawless Consulting: A Guide to Getting Your Expertise Used*. Though initially a solo work, Block's book laid the foundation for countless collaborative workshops, certification programs, and consulting alliances.

As the book gained traction, it attracted consulting professionals, HR leaders, and organizational development experts who wanted to partner, teach, or build on the methodology.

This kind of co-creation and shared expertise enhances credibility and dramatically increases reach. For consultants, co-authoring or collaborating deeply on book content—whether it's research, case studies, or frameworks—can lead to webinars, panel discussions, training programs, and even firm-level partnerships.

Increasing Referrals and Recommendations

Beyond direct collaborations, a book also acts as a powerful referral engine. When clients, peers, or industry professionals find genuine value in your writing, they're far more likely to recommend your services to others. It becomes easier for them to *vouch* for you because they have something tangible to reference: your published ideas.

In consulting, where trust and expertise are non-negotiable, a well-written book serves as social proof of credibility. It reassures potential clients and collaborators of your depth and professionalism.

Over time, this can lead to organic growth in your network, with new business inquiries, partnership proposals, and speaking invitations coming your way—not through cold outreach, but through word of mouth and credible recommendations.

For consultants, authorship isn't just a branding exercise. It's a magnet for the right kinds of professional relationships—ones that lead to meaningful collaborations, steady referrals, and sustained growth.

Media and PR Opportunities

You've probably noticed consultants in your industry gaining more visibility, not necessarily because they know more than you, but because they've written a book. Even if your expertise runs deeper, the moment someone adds "author" or "bestselling author" to their title, they're more likely to be invited for interviews, quoted in articles, or featured on expert panels. That's the power of positioning—and a book gives you that edge.

In the world of consulting, credibility is currency. And one of the fastest ways to establish that credibility in the eyes of the media is to author a book on your area of expertise. The moment you do, media outreach becomes significantly easier. Journalists, podcast hosts, and event organizers are more likely to feature someone who has published original thinking, especially when it's presented in the form of a professional book.

This isn't just theory—data backs it. Studies have shown that only a small fraction of consultants and thought leaders publish a book, with estimates suggesting that fewer than 5% do so. Yet, those who do often enjoy a disproportionately higher share of attention, influence, and inbound opportunities. Let's call them *The Top 5%*. These are the voices that appear on conference stages, in business magazines, and on industry podcasts. Their secret isn't necessarily superior expertise—it's authorship.

When you write a book, you give the media a compelling reason to reach out to *you*. It becomes easier to secure interviews, guest columns, and expert commentary slots. This kind of exposure doesn't just boost your reputation—it extends your professional reach, helping you connect with a broader audience of potential clients, collaborators, and decision-makers.

For consultants, media attention can be a game-changer. It amplifies the impact of your existing network and expands access to people and platforms you might never have reached through conventional networking alone. And the gateway to that visibility? A book with your name on it.

For consultants, credibility is everything. It's the foundation of trust with clients, peers, and the industry as a whole.

Writing a book instantly elevates that credibility. It sends a clear signal that you're not just doing the work—you've thought deeply about it, refined your insights, and are ready to share your expertise with the world.

Think of it this way: imagine you're a consultant with a unique methodology or a transformative client success story. You've turned that experience into a well-written, insightful book that outlines your process, the results, and the lessons learned. This book becomes more than a showcase of your capabilities—it becomes a compelling narrative about your professional journey and the value you bring.

Now, here's where the PR opportunity comes in. Business and industry publications are always on the lookout for fresh content, especially stories that blend innovation, leadership, and insight. Your book gives your publicist (or even you) the perfect angle to pitch to media platforms. It's no longer a cold introduction—now there's a hook: a consultant with a breakthrough idea, backed by a published book.

Once your book is out, it becomes a media asset. Magazines, podcasts, and business blogs may feature you, not just because of the book, but because the book offers a structured, engaging entry point into your work. These features boost your profile and establish you as a credible voice in your niche.

Each mention—whether it's a guest column, a podcast interview, or a short profile in a trade publication—compounds your visibility. And here's the best part: the media doesn't just talk about the book once. Your book will become a valuable reference point in future interviews, panel discussions, and client conversations. It's something people can quote, link to, and return to again and again.

In essence, your book becomes the cornerstone of your PR engine. For consultants aiming to grow their brand, expand their reach, and become go-to experts in their field, authorship isn't just a milestone—it's a multiplier.

Key Takeaways:

- **A Book as a Strategic Networking Asset:** Writing a book gives consultants a powerful, tangible way to showcase their expertise. It serves as a natural conversation starter and positions you as a trusted voice, making it easier to build meaningful professional connections.

- **Increased Access to Speaking Opportunities:** As an author, you're more likely to be invited to speak at industry events, workshops, and corporate panels. These platforms enhance your visibility, boost your reputation, and connect you with broader, high-value audiences.

- **Pathway to Collaboration:** A published book signals authority, making you a more attractive partner for co-authored projects, joint ventures, or consulting alliances. It opens doors to working alongside other experts and thought leaders.

- **Boost in Referrals and Credibility:** When people read and trust your ideas, they're more likely to recommend your services. A book helps build that trust and credibility, naturally increasing client referrals and peer endorsements.

- **Enhanced Media and PR Reach:** Authorship can attract the attention of media outlets, podcasts, and professional blogs, thereby increasing your visibility and credibility. It becomes easier to land interviews, be featured in expert roundups, and grow your influence beyond your immediate circle.

***

4

The Fear of Being Seen

"The single greatest "people skill" is a highly developed & authentic interest in the other person."

——**Bob Burg**

Trust turns a one-time project into a long-term engagement. It's what transforms a cold pitch into a strategic partnership. And in a marketplace saturated with consultants all promising results, trust is what sets you apart.

But how do you build trust beyond the day-to-day interactions? Beyond the slide decks and workshops? How do you leave a lasting impression that extends far past the confines of the meeting room? Now, imagine this scene. You've just wrapped up a strategic review session. You may have spent the past two hours walking a client's executive team through a complex transformation roadmap. The room is full of decision-makers; some skeptical, some intrigued, some cautiously optimistic. You've fielded tough questions, defended your assumptions, and outlined the path forward. As the meeting winds down, there's a natural pause. This is the moment when, traditionally, a consultant hands over a business card, perhaps a follow-up email summarizing next steps, or maybe a nicely formatted case study.

But you do something different. You reach into your bag and hand the CEO a copy of your book. A real, tangible book, with your name on the cover and your thinking captured across its chapters. You say, "Much of what we discussed today is explored in more depth here. I thought this might be useful as you continue to lead your organization through change."

The gesture is small, almost understated. But the impact is profound.

In that moment, you shift from being a service provider to a thought leader. From someone who solves problems on a project basis to someone who has invested years thinking about the very challenges your clients face. Your book becomes more than a takeaway—it becomes a representation of your credibility, your philosophy, and your commitment to your craft.

Think about what this signals to the room. First, it demonstrates that you've taken the time to distill your ideas and frameworks into something enduring. Second, it reflects transparency—you are opening up your intellectual process, inviting others to examine, question, and apply your thinking. Additionally, it demonstrates a long-term orientation. You didn't write a book overnight. You wrote it because your commitment to this domain goes beyond billable hours and project deliverables. This is your life's work. Stakeholders notice that. And they respect it.

This scenario isn't theoretical. It is a real-world strategy employed by consultants who understand that in the modern marketplace, authority is earned through contribution, not self-promotion. These consultants have leveraged their books to deepen trust with existing clients, open doors to new prospects, and foster peer-level conversations with executives who might otherwise view consultants as transactional vendors.

A well-written book changes the dynamics of a relationship. It levels the playing field. Suddenly, you're not just delivering a service—you're shaping the conversation around the service. Clients stop seeing you as someone who executes strategies and start seeing you as someone who influences how strategies are designed in the first place. It's the difference between advising on a digital transformation initiative and helping redefine what digital transformation means in your industry.

Beyond clients, your book also plays a decisive role in your broader professional ecosystem. Collaborators, partners, industry peers—these relationships, too, are built on trust. When you publish a book, you create opportunities for deeper engagement with this network.

Picture a fellow consultant, someone whose work you admire, reading your book and reaching out to discuss a shared challenge. What begins as mutual respect evolves into a collaboration on a webinar, a co-authored article, or a joint client engagement. Your book has facilitated not just connection, but meaningful collaboration.

Or imagine a conference organizer searching for speakers who bring fresh, actionable insights to their audience. They come across your book, are impressed by the depth of your thinking, and invite you to lead a keynote session. That one invitation expands your professional circle, introduces you to hundreds of potential collaborators and clients, and solidifies your position as a thought leader in your domain.

This is how relationships grow in the modern consulting world, not through hard sells, but through shared ideas and mutual value creation.

And it's not only about the high-profile opportunities. Sometimes, the most meaningful connections are forged in quiet moments. Like when a client emails you months after a project concludes, saying, "I finally finished your book over the weekend. It gave me a new way of thinking about our organizational culture. Can we schedule some time to discuss how we might revisit our strategy?" That conversation wouldn't happen because you followed up relentlessly. It would happen because your book was there when they were ready. After all, books have a long shelf life. They sit on desks, in briefcases, and on nightstands, waiting for the right moment to spark action.

You can showcase your work in a manner that a presentation deck cannot, i.e., without limited space to explain the 'why' behind your frameworks. In your book, you can take the reader on the whole journey, sharing the context, the failures, the lessons learned, and the nuanced thinking that shaped your conclusions. This transparency builds trust in a way that polished recommendations alone cannot.

Clients don't just want answers. They want to know how you arrived at those answers. They want to see your thought process, your methodology, and your rigor. A book provides that window.

And while books are traditionally one-way communication, in the consulting world, they spark dialogue. Clients read your chapter on leadership alignment and want to debate its applications in their organization. Partners read your case studies and suggest ways to extend your frameworks into new industries. Peers challenge your assumptions, sharpening your thinking through healthy discourse.

Your book becomes a catalyst for meaningful conversations. And through those conversations, relationships evolve from transactional to transformational. You're no longer seen as just a vendor filling a service gap. You're seen as a partner in your clients' growth; someone who is invested in their success beyond the terms of a contract.

This is what creates client loyalty. Not because you discount your fees or over-deliver on hours, but because you've shown that your expertise is rooted in genuine curiosity and continuous learning.

Over time, your book helps you cultivate a professional brand built on trust, transparency, and thought leadership. When new opportunities arise, you're not just another consultant in the pipeline. You're the author who helped shape the industry's conversation on resilience, change, or innovation.

Of course, none of this happens overnight. Trust is not a marketing tactic. It is earned slowly, consistently, and authentically. But your book accelerates the journey. It creates a shortcut to credibility, allowing stakeholders to engage with your thinking deeply and on their terms. This doesn't mean your book has to be perfect. It needs to be honest, insightful, and valuable. Stakeholders don't expect literary brilliance from a consultant-author. They expect clarity, relevance, and sincerity. They want to learn something practical and applicable. They want to feel that your book was written with them in mind, not simply to boost your profile.

And perhaps most importantly, your book shows that you are in this for the long haul. You are not a consultant chasing the successive quick win.

You are someone who has committed years to studying your domain, refining your craft, and sharing your insights with the world.

That long-term orientation is rare and deeply valued.

Ultimately, consulting is a human endeavor. No matter how advanced your frameworks, how sophisticated your tools, or how data-driven your recommendations, clients and partners will always choose to work with people they trust. People who show up authentically. People who care.

Your book allows you to show up in that way, long before the first meeting, and long after the engagement concludes. The next time you wrap up a project or prepare for a critical pitch, consider what you leave behind. A polished deck is expected. A business card is forgotten. But a book that stays. It stays on their desk, reminding them of your conversation. It stays in their mind, influencing how they approach their next challenge. It stays in their network and is passed along to a colleague who says, "This is exactly what we've been talking about in our leadership offsite."

And in that staying power lies your most fabulous opportunity—to build relationships that endure. Relationships that are rooted not in what you sell, but in what you contribute.

That is the essence of trust in consulting. And that is the legacy of your book.

Enhancing Communication Skills

For consultants, effective communication is at the heart of every successful engagement. Writing a book can be a transformative tool in refining how you convey complex ideas to clients, stakeholders, and broader audiences. It enables you to present your vision, clarify your approach, and address frequently asked questions in a thoughtful and structured format.

The discipline of writing sharpens your ability to explain nuanced concepts in a way that resonates with both technical and non-technical audiences. This skill pays off immensely during client presentations, workshops, and stakeholder meetings. Authorship also requires you to step into the shoes of your reader, whether that reader is a CEO, a procurement head, or a mid-level manager. By anticipating their questions and concerns, you learn to frame your ideas with empathy and clarity.

This heightened awareness helps you become more effective in tailoring your messaging to different types of stakeholders, a key consulting competency.

These skills directly translate to improved communication in client settings, where clarity, effective feedback integration, and message alignment are essential to success.

In essence, writing a book isn't just about showcasing expertise—it's a rigorous exercise in improving how you express that expertise. For consultants, this leads to clearer client deliverables, stronger proposals, and more persuasive conversations.

Marshall Goldsmith, one of the world's top executive coaches and leadership consultants, transformed his professional brand and influence through the power of authorship. With decades of consulting experience, Goldsmith chose to share his insights in his bestselling book *What Got You Here Won't Get You There*. Rooted in real executive coaching challenges, the book distilled his methodologies into accessible, relatable content that resonated with a global audience.

By writing this book, Goldsmith did more than document his experience—he provided a transparent and structured explanation of his consulting approach and coaching philosophy. The book became a communication tool not just for marketing but also for aligning expectations with stakeholders—CEOs, HR heads, boards, and even the executives he coached directly. It helped clients understand his value before the first conversation and served as a reference point throughout the consulting engagement.

Goldsmith's book helped him connect with a broader network of decision-makers, positioning him as a go-to expert in leadership development. For stakeholders, having a tangible representation of his process created trust and confidence—it showed clarity of thought, a tested approach, and a deep understanding of organizational dynamics. Completing and publishing a book gave Goldsmith an added layer of credibility—not just with clients but within the broader consulting and leadership communities.

Translating his frameworks and experiences into written form sharpened his communication skills and provided a medium to address common leadership challenges in detail.

This publication boosted his self-assurance and opened new professional pathways—from keynote speeches to global coaching programs and media appearances. As industry leaders and readers engaged with his work, the feedback reinforced his authority and validated the years of consulting experience he brought to the table.

For consultants, this case demonstrates that writing a book isn't just about personal branding—it's about codifying your expertise in a way that builds stakeholder trust, enhances your visibility, and deepens your conviction in your ideas. It's not the end of your consulting journey—it's the point where your influence begins to scale.

One of the biggest challenges for consultants is answering the same stakeholder questions repeatedly with clarity and consistency. Whether it's a prospective client inquiring about your process or a partner uncertain about your value proposition, those initial conversations often set the tone for the relationship.

That's where a book becomes a powerful asset. A well-crafted book functions like a long-form FAQ, addressing key questions your audience may have about your consulting model, methodology, or results. Instead of repeating explanations, your book offers a structured, thoughtful response—one that positions you as a prepared and authoritative expert.

A prime example of this in action is David A. Fields, a successful consultant and author of *The Irresistible Consultant's Guide to Winning Clients*. Fields wrote the book to help other consultants understand how to structure and grow their practices. In doing so, he also created a valuable resource that addressed all the common questions potential clients and peers had about his approach.

By walking readers through his client-centric philosophy, pricing strategies, and relationship management techniques, Fields used the book to eliminate ambiguity.

The clarity and transparency of his ideas not only saved him time in conversations but also built trust with those seeking his guidance. Readers who came across his book often reached out, already aligned with his worldview, having had their concerns addressed before the first meeting.

For consultants, writing a book is an efficient way to streamline stakeholder education. You can explain your approach, highlight your principles, and preemptively clarify common misunderstandings without having to do it in every client conversation. It's not just a tool for marketing—it's a way to improve your consulting relationships before they even begin.

Building Trust and Loyalty

Trust is the foundation of every strong consulting relationship, especially in a field where clients often make high-stakes decisions based on your advice. A book can play a vital role in establishing that trust by demonstrating your expertise, transparency, and commitment to delivering value.

While writing and refining a book takes time, reflection, and rigorous thought, the payoff is substantial. Your book becomes a testament to your knowledge and a signal of your professionalism. It allows potential clients, collaborators, and stakeholders to get to know your perspective, approach, and values, long before you ever enter the boardroom.

For consultants, a book isn't just a credibility booster; it's a tool to deepen loyalty. It shows that you care enough about your field to document your ideas and share them thoughtfully. It conveys that you're committed to helping others succeed, not just in closing deals.

As your book circulates, it helps you expand your visibility, attract aligned clients, and foster deeper engagement. Over time, it accelerates the growth of your practice, not through aggressive selling, but through the quiet confidence that comes from earned trust.

In essence, consultants who write books don't just build their brand—they build relationships. In consulting, strong relationships are the primary drivers of long-term success.

Demonstrating Commitment to Transparency and Thought Leadership

Writing a book as a consultant is not just a marketing strategy—it's a bold declaration of your commitment to your practice and your clients. It takes time, energy, and deep reflection, signaling to the world that you take your expertise seriously and are willing to share it with clarity and honesty.

By documenting your consulting journey—your frameworks, challenges, breakthroughs, and real-world client experiences—you show stakeholders that you operate with transparency. A well-written book allows you to articulate your unique philosophy, shed light on your decision-making process, and demonstrate the values that guide your professional approach. That level of openness builds trust and positions you as a leader in your field.

More than a personal branding tool, a book becomes a platform for establishing absolute authority. When you put your insights, strategies, and hard-earned lessons into print, you offer a tangible representation of your knowledge, one that your peers, clients, and prospective partners can engage with long after the initial encounter.

A strong book can attract attention from other consultants, business leaders, and industry insiders who resonate with your ideas. This can open doors to professional relationships, client referrals, or even cross-disciplinary collaborations. It's not uncommon for consultants who author books to receive invitations to speak at conferences, contribute to expert panels, or be featured in media outlets—all of which further cement their reputation as thought leaders.

Perhaps most importantly, your book becomes part of your professional legacy. It serves as a resource for future consultants, clients, and changemakers who may learn from your perspective. By contributing to the intellectual fabric of your industry, you elevate not only your own practice but also the field as a whole.

Writing a book is one of the most powerful moves consultants can make if they want to lead with clarity, inspire trust, and leave a lasting impact.

Case Study: Bernadette Jiwa and "Make Your Idea Matter"

Bernadette Jiwa, a globally recognized brand storytelling consultant, authored *Make Your Idea Matter* to help entrepreneurs and organizations articulate the "why" behind their work. In doing so, she didn't just offer a marketing guide—she gave the consulting world a transparent look into her philosophy and the principles she uses to help brands connect meaningfully with their audiences.

By candidly sharing her methods, client experiences, and core beliefs, Jiwa built immediate credibility with potential clients and industry peers. Her book addresses common questions about brand messaging, market relevance, and customer connection—topics consultants in branding and communication are frequently asked to navigate. It served not just as a how-to guide, but as a clear demonstration of her thinking and values.

Her openness about what works—and what doesn't—reinforced her commitment to honesty, creativity, and making a positive impact. It also showed that she wasn't selling fluff; she was offering proven, deeply considered insight. This transparency strengthened her relationships with current clients and earned her trust with new ones before the first conversation even began.

Make Your Idea Matter helped elevate Jiwa's reputation globally, leading to keynote invitations, consulting projects with major brands, and recognition as a leading voice in her niche. The book became her calling card, a credibility builder that lived beyond meetings and pitches.

For consultants, Jiwa's journey is a testament to what's possible when you package your expertise into a thoughtful, honest book. It's a tool to demonstrate leadership, attract aligned clients, and build a lasting reputation grounded in trust, clarity, and contribution.

Enhancing Relationships with Clients

Clients are at the center of any consulting business, and trust is the currency that drives long-term engagements. A well-written book helps you deepen client relationships by showcasing your expertise, addressing common concerns, and offering solutions grounded in real-world experience.

Example: Blair Enns and The Win Without Pitching Manifesto

Blair Enns, a business development consultant for creative firms, authored *The Win Without Pitching Manifesto* to challenge traditional ways agencies and consultants pitch for business. Instead of giving away ideas for free, Enns advocates for value-based selling and positioning oneself as a trusted advisor. His book resonates deeply with clients by addressing a shared pain point—pricing and positioning in a competitive market. By clearly laying out his approach and the philosophy behind it, Enns builds instant credibility with prospective clients. The book acts as both an onboarding tool and a trust accelerator, helping clients understand his methods before the first conversation even begins.

Enhancing Relationships with Employees and Teams

While consultants may not have employees in the traditional sense, many lead small teams, collaborate with contractors, or work within larger client ecosystems. Writing a book can help clarify your leadership style and values, aligning everyone involved around a shared mission and approach to work.

Example: David H. Maister and True Professionalism

David Maister, a former Harvard Business School professor turned consultant, wrote *"True Professionalism"* to guide professionals—especially those in consulting, legal, and accounting firms—on the values and mindset needed to thrive in client-facing roles.

In doing so, Maister didn't just reach clients—he connected with junior consultants, internal teams, and partners.

His book helps align teams on what "professionalism" truly means: integrity, client focus, and personal responsibility. By openly sharing his philosophy, Maister has built stronger bonds within his consulting circles and left a legacy that continues to influence team dynamics in professional services firms worldwide.

Building Relationships with the Wider Community

Consultants also operate within a larger professional ecosystem, comprising fellow consultants, industry influencers, potential collaborators, and the general public. Writing a book enables you to make a meaningful contribution to this community, expanding your influence and deepening your industry footprint.

Example: Roger L. Martin and Playing to Win

Roger L. Martin, former Dean of the Rotman School of Management and strategic advisor to major corporations, co-authored *Playing to Win* with P&G's A.G. Lafley. The book outlines a practical approach to strategy that consultants across disciplines reference in their work.

Martin's transparency in sharing strategic frameworks and real corporate case studies has earned him the respect of his peers and expanded his audience far beyond academia or boardrooms. His work now influences thousands of consultants and strategists globally, fostering a vast network of engagement and collaboration.

Key Takeaways:

- **Improving Communication:** A book allows consultants to articulate their frameworks, methodologies, and perspectives clearly. It serves as a comprehensive medium for conveying your consulting approach, addressing client concerns.

- **Building Trust and Loyalty:** A book helps establish credibility and authenticity by transparently sharing your expertise, process, and guiding principles. This openness builds long-term trust and loyalty among clients.

- **Enhancing Relationships with Clients:** Your book offers clients a deeper understanding of your value proposition, strategic thinking, and problem-solving approach. It reassures them of your credibility and helps them engage with your ideas .

- **Strengthening Connections with Teams and Collaborators:** For consultants who work with internal teams, partners, or networks, a book can communicate your professional values, leadership style, and expectations.

***

5

Personal And Professional Fulfilment

"The best way to predict the future is to create it."

———**Peter Drucker**

In the hyper-competitive arena of consulting, where markets evolve rapidly and competitors emerge seemingly overnight, your reputation is often your strongest—and sometimes your only—differentiator. Unlike a product-based business where differentiation might rest on price points, features, or patents, the consulting world runs on something far more intangible yet far more powerful: trust in your expertise. This trust is not built solely on the number of clients you've worked with or the logos you display on your website. Those things help, yes, but they are table stakes in a world where most consultants have similar credentials and overlapping skill sets. True differentiation happens when your name becomes synonymous with clarity, leadership, and original thinking. And few tools accelerate that process more powerfully than a book.

Picture yourself entering a new market, perhaps you're expanding your consulting practice to a region where no one knows your name. You're launching a new service offering, a new methodology, or an entire vertical that you want to build authority in.

What's your first move?

Most consultants default to familiar tactics: pitch decks, white papers, webinars, maybe some strategic networking. These tools are helpful, but they are expected.

They help you join the conversation, but rarely do they help you lead it. Now, imagine taking a different approach.

Imagine walking into that same market not with a generic presentation, but with a published book in your hands. A book that doesn't just outline your services but articulates your consulting philosophy, your frameworks, your client success stories, and your bold vision for transforming business outcomes. A book that speaks directly to the challenges your target market is facing and offers a path forward. Immediately, the dynamic changes.

You are no longer simply a consultant competing for attention. You are an author shaping the dialogue. You are an authority with a point of view, not just a service to sell. Potential clients, instead of seeing another pitch deck, encounter a thoughtful body of work that demonstrates the depth of your thinking. They gain insight into how you approach problems, what principles guide your work, and why your solutions produce results. Before you've had a single project briefing, they've already begun to trust your expertise.

But the ripple effect doesn't stop there. Media outlets, industry blogs, and podcasts are constantly on the lookout for fresh voices—individuals who can shed light on emerging trends, challenge conventional thinking, and offer new frameworks for tackling persistent problems. A book makes it easy for them to find you.

Consider the journalist covering leadership innovation in Fortune 500 companies. They're looking for someone who can comment on the shifting dynamics of executive teams in the digital age. Your book—perhaps titled *Leading Through Disruption: A Consultant's Guide to the New Executive Playbook*—lands on their radar. Within days, you're quoted in a feature story that reaches thousands of decision-makers you've never met.

Or think about the podcast producer curating speakers for a series on business transformation. Your book's thoughtful take on change management resonates with their audience's interests. You're invited for an interview, where your message reaches listeners during their morning commutes and late-night brainstorming sessions.

That exposure, earned through the quality of your thinking, places you in circles you couldn't access through networking alone.

What's happening here is a credibility multiplier. Your book isn't just expanding your audience; it's deepening your influence. It turns passive awareness into active trust. It signals to the market that you are not just practicing consulting—you are influencing how consulting is practiced. In an industry where ideas are your currency, that influence is priceless. Now, some may argue that reputation in consulting is built through doing, not publishing. Indeed, your track record of successful client engagements forms the backbone of your credibility. But here's the reality: the market only knows what you show them. No matter how transformational your past projects were, if those stories and lessons remain confined to confidential decks and closed-door conversations, your reputation will never extend beyond your immediate network.

A book changes that. It pulls back the curtain on your work, not in a way that compromises client confidentiality, but in a way that shares the universal lessons, frameworks, and philosophies you've refined through years of practice. It's one thing to say, "I help organizations navigate complex transformations." It's another thing entirely to show, chapter by chapter, how transformation unfolds, why it fails, and what truly makes it sustainable. That level of transparency and thought leadership turns a transactional relationship into a strategic one. It's what makes a prospective client say, "This is the person we need to lead our next big initiative."

The best part? Your book continues working for you while you sleep. It sits on executives' bookshelves, is shared among leadership teams, and appears on industry reading lists. It circulates far beyond your direct reach, introducing you to people and opportunities you may never have known existed.

This isn't just a theoretical outcome. Many of the world's most respected consultants have built their reputations this way. Names like Patrick Lencioni, Marshall Goldsmith, and Ram Charan didn't become household names in executive suites because they waited for clients to spread the word about them.

They wrote books that framed how entire industries think about leadership, performance, and strategy. And they started exactly where you are: with an idea, an insight, and the courage to put their thinking on paper.

You don't have to be a global guru to experience the benefits. Even within your niche market or specialization, a book can establish you as the go-to voice. Whether you consult in financial services, healthcare, tech startups, or family-owned businesses, your book gives you a platform that few competitors are willing—or able—to build.

Reputation today is not only about who you know but about who knows you. And often, the first time a potential client "meets" you is not in a boardroom but through your ideas. They might read your book on a flight, quote your frameworks in a leadership retreat, or discuss your chapter in a peer roundtable long before they ever pick up the phone to call you.

By the time they do, the sales process feels less like a cold pitch and more like a natural next step in an ongoing conversation. You've already established trust. You've already demonstrated value. The book has done the introduction for you.

In crowded consulting markets where every firm claims to drive results, differentiation is subtle yet powerful. It's in the way you frame problems differently. It's in the vision you paint for what's possible. It's in your willingness to share your thinking openly, inviting dialogue rather than guarding your insights behind paywalls and proposals.

A book, at its best, becomes a manifesto for how you believe your industry can evolve. It articulates not only what you do but why you do it—and why that matters. In doing so, it attracts clients who resonate with your philosophy, peers who want to collaborate, and talent who want to join your mission.

The question, then, is not whether a book can elevate your reputation. The question is whether you are willing to step into that role.

Writing a book demands vulnerability. You are putting your ideas out into the world where they can be debated, critiqued, and—if you've done your job well—implemented. That requires courage. But it also offers the extraordinary reward of knowing that your work is not confined to project timelines and quarterly reports. Your ideas have a life of their own.

And isn't that what many consultants ultimately seek? To leave a mark. To influence not only the clients they serve but the industry they belong to. To be remembered not only for the projects they delivered but for the conversations they helped shape. When you publish a book, you are making a public commitment to your craft. You are saying, "These ideas matter. This work matters. And I'm willing to be part of the solution."

In a marketplace where noise is abundant and attention spans are short, a book is a statement of depth. It's a reminder that thoughtful, well-crafted insight still has a place. It's proof that you've done the hard work of reflection, synthesis, and articulation.

And while articles, podcasts, and social media posts all play a role in modern thought leadership, a book remains the gold standard. It is the anchor that holds your professional narrative together.

So, as you look to build your consulting brand—whether in a new market, a new vertical, or simply on a larger stage—ask yourself: will you compete on noise, or will you compete on clarity? Will you be another voice in the crowd, or the one with a message that lasts?

Your book gives you that message. It doesn't just speak for you when you're not in the room. It opens doors you never knew existed. It turns introductions into conversations, conversations into trust, and trust into opportunities. And in a world where credibility is the currency of influence, that makes all the difference.

Marketing and Branding for Consultants

Unlike traditional marketing materials, a book offers consultants a powerful and deeply engaging way to communicate their personal brand, consulting philosophy, and core values. It provides nuance and context that a LinkedIn post or credentials deck simply cannot, creating more personal and meaningful engagement with your audience.

That makes it an essential pillar of any modern marketing strategy for both independent consultants and consulting firms.

Publishing a book isn't just about getting noticed—it's about getting trusted. It serves as a multifunctional tool that supports nearly every business goal, including increasing visibility, generating media attention, building thought leadership, attracting clients, and reinforcing credibility. In a competitive field where differentiation is difficult, a book gives you authority on paper—and in perception.

Leveraging Your Book for Consulting Practice Growth and Brand Building

For consultants, a book can serve as a transformative asset, far beyond just pages of content. It becomes a strategic tool for growing your consulting practice and building a personal or firm-level brand that stands out in a saturated market. By sharing your unique methodologies, case studies, and insights, you can attract high-value clients, collaborators, and even corporate partners who align with your approach and values.

A well-received book can change the trajectory of your career. It can open doors to new industries, establish credibility with C-suite decision-makers, and initiate conversations that would otherwise require years of networking to access. For many consultants, it becomes a natural bridge to additional ventures like executive education, keynote speaking, licensing of IP, and even transitioning into full-time advisory or teaching roles.

Beyond traditional book sales, the content of your book can evolve into multiple revenue streams, including online courses, private workshops, paid newsletters, consulting toolkits, or exclusive memberships. These extensions not only expand your income potential but also amplify your influence and brand equity in the consulting space.

Books also travel where you can't—reaching global audiences, entering corporate boardrooms, and being shared among industry influencers.

Your ideas gain a life of their own, influencing decision-making and positioning you as a global authority in your niche. The reach of a book often exceeds that of any single engagement or marketing campaign.

Writing a book is not just a one-time project—it's a career catalyst. It acts as your ambassador, signaling expertise, building visibility, establishing thought leadership, opening up high-impact speaking opportunities, and reinforcing your authority across multiple touchpoints. A book becomes your lodestar, guiding your growth, reputation, and professional legacy.

Becoming a Go-To Expert for Media and Thought Leadership

Publishing a book as a consultant positions you as a trusted authority in your field, making you a natural choice for interviews, expert commentary, and guest contributions in industry publications. Media outlets and journalists regularly seek out authors for their insights, and having your name on the cover of a well-regarded book signals depth, credibility, and relevance.

Being recognized as an expert can also lead to invitations to platforms that not only expand your influence but also put you in direct contact with other leaders, decision-makers, and potential clients or partners. Each public engagement enhances your credibility and visibility, thereby reinforcing your reputation within the consulting community.

Media appearances and expert quotes in respected publications can also funnel attention to your consulting website, lead magnets, or digital presence, boosting brand awareness and lead generation. When a consultant is seen as a thought leader, clients are far more likely to trust their methodology and pay a premium for their services.

Using Your Book to Drive Content Marketing as a Consultant

For consultants, a book is not just a standalone product—it's a content goldmine. Every page you write becomes a well of ideas, frameworks, stories, and strategies that can be repurposed across multiple marketing channels to boost your visibility, attract leads, and strengthen your brand.

By turning chapters or key insights into blog posts, newsletter series, LinkedIn carousel posts, or even lead magnets like whitepapers and templates, you extend the life and reach of your intellectual property. This not only reinforces your thought leadership but also ensures that your voice stays consistent and credible across platforms.

Each blog post based on your book can dive deeper into a niche subject, demonstrating your domain expertise. Sharing these insights improves SEO and brings more organic traffic to your consulting website. Meanwhile, posting quotes, key takeaways, and practical tips from your book on LinkedIn or X (formerly Twitter) provides daily opportunities for engagement with your professional network.

You can also build a webinar series or a podcast inspired by your book. These formats enable you to engage your audience in real-time, answer questions, and showcase your consulting approach in action, helping potential clients understand your value before they ever schedule a sales call. Repurposing your book into audiovisual content adds a human element to your messaging, building trust more quickly.

Downloadable e-books, infographics, and lead magnets derived from your book content can be powerful tools for lead generation. According to *Forbes*, creating free educational resources based on original thought leadership significantly increases email sign-ups and inbound consulting inquiries.

Example: Michael Bungay Stanier and The Coaching Habit

Michael Bungay Stanier, a consultant and founder of Box of Crayons, transformed his book, *The Coaching Habit: Say Less, Ask More & Change the Way You Lead Forever*, into a comprehensive content ecosystem. Beyond selling hundreds of thousands of copies, Stanier used the book's frameworks to generate blog posts, downloadable tools, online courses, YouTube content, and even corporate training modules.

By repurposing the material, he created an ongoing stream of relevant, high-value content that helped organizations better understand the role of coaching in the workplace. This expanded his firm's reach and established Box of Crayons as a premier coaching-based consulting company, serving major clients such as Microsoft and TD Bank.

For consultants, your book is the fuel for an entire marketing engine. It helps you stay consistent, amplify your message, and remain top-of-mind in your industry. You don't need to keep inventing new content—you need to extract and adapt what you've already put into the book.

Establishing Thought Leadership as a Consultant

For consultants, establishing yourself as a thought leader is not just a branding move—it's a strategic imperative. In a field where credibility, trust, and expertise are your core assets, publishing a book becomes one of the most effective ways to *show*, not just *tell*, your authority.

A well-written book distills your consulting experience, frameworks, insights, and case studies into a timeless resource. It does more than showcase your thinking—it proves that you've done the work, refined your perspective, and have something original to contribute to your industry. When clients, peers, or media see your name on a published book, you're no longer just one of many consultants—they now see you as *a published expert*.

Unlike momentary blog posts or fleeting social media content, books have a long-lasting impact. They become reference points for teams, leaders, and decision-makers long after the initial release. Your book can be handed out at conferences, sent to clients, referenced in meetings, and passed down through networks, creating compounding visibility.

A published book serves as a permanent addition to your intellectual legacy. It documents your methodologies, philosophies, and frameworks in a structured, shareable form. This becomes particularly powerful when you scale your business or transition into roles such as keynote speaker, executive coach, or advisor.

The ideas you publish can inform policy, influence corporate training, and shape how organizations approach problems—even when you're not in the room.

Example: David C. Baker and The Business of Expertise

David C. Baker, a seasoned consultant to creative firms, wrote *The Business of Expertise* to distill decades of experience into a concise, impactful guide. Throughout the book, he shared clear frameworks on positioning, pricing, and strategy that directly addressed the needs of independent consultants and small firms.

The book didn't just build Baker's reputation—it extended his influence across industries. It led to more keynote opportunities, podcast interviews, guest lectures, and higher-value clients. His firm became synonymous with clarity and focus, and his writing continues to educate consultants worldwide long after publication.

For consultants, a book is not just a calling card—it's a legacy artifact. It preserves their thinking, shapes the next generation of professionals, and builds long-term equity in their personal and professional brand.

By writing a book, you move from being a service provider to a recognized authority whose influence endures. You don't just market your expertise—you memorialize it, and in doing so, *lead your field*.

Creating Long-Term Impact and Broad Reach Through Your Book

For consultants, a book is not just a marketing tool—it's a legacy-building instrument. Unlike social media posts, webinars, or newsletters that fade with the feed, a well-written book endures. It possesses a unique ability to reach a broad and diverse audience, often long after its original publication date.

Books remain discoverable through libraries, bookstores, search engines, and academic databases.

This means your expertise continues to find new audiences over the years, not just days or weeks. Whether it's an executive seeking guidance, a consultant looking for strategic insights, or a client exploring your methodology, your book becomes a permanent resource that builds your brand even when you're not actively promoting it.

Beyond the business world, your book may be adopted in educational and professional settings—from MBA classrooms to consulting certification courses. Many consultants have seen their books used in university curricula, corporate training programs, and leadership workshops, thereby influencing how future professionals think, work, and lead.

Creating Long-Term Impact

For consultants, a book is not just a marketing asset—it's a legacy of knowledge. Unlike blog posts or webinars that disappear into the content stream, a book has longevity. It remains discoverable and valuable for years, becoming a go-to reference in your field and shaping industry thinking long after publication.

By writing a book, consultants encapsulate their unique frameworks, methodologies, and perspectives into a format that transcends time and geography. This long-term influence enhances credibility, keeps their ideas in circulation, and solidifies their voice in conversations they may not even be present for.

Case Study: Cal Newport and Deep Work

Cal Newport may not call himself a "consultant" in the traditional sense, but his work has profoundly influenced productivity consultants, executive coaches, and performance strategists across industries. A computer science professor by training, Newport wrote *Deep Work: Rules for Focused Success in a Distracted World* in 2016—a book that crystallized the philosophy of deep, focused cognitive work over the noise of constant distractions.

Since its publication, *Deep Work* has been widely adopted by consulting firms, leadership coaches, and organizational development experts. It's referenced in C-suite strategy workshops, employee training programs, and enterprise productivity audits. Newport's framework has inspired consultants to develop new client offerings, restructure how companies measure performance, and even redesign internal policies around meetings and communication.

His book didn't just share ideas—it created a movement around deep focus. Consultants around the world now build on Newport's insights to help teams reclaim their time, attention, and creative energy. Nearly a decade later, *Deep Work* still shapes conversations in both tech and corporate consulting arenas.

Why This Matters for Consultants

When you write a book as a consultant, you don't just share what you know—you create a toolkit others will use, cite, and build upon. It becomes the foundation for new conversations, new contracts, and even new careers.

A lasting book helps:

- Future-proof your brand by ensuring your name remains relevant in industry discussions.

- Expand your influence as readers share your ideas with clients, peers, and leaders.

- Open new income streams through speaking, training, licensing, or consulting packages based on your book's IP.

Books outlast business cards, portfolios, and sales decks. They are portable authorities.

Creating a Legacy

As a consultant, your expertise is built over years of client interactions, problem-solving, strategy development, and organizational transformation. But unless it's documented, much of this insight remains confined to boardrooms, presentations, or internal reports. Writing a book enables you to transform your lived experiences into a lasting legacy.

A book becomes a tangible asset—a structured, enduring reflection of your thinking, methods, and unique perspective on the consulting profession. It's more than just personal branding. It's your contribution to the broader body of knowledge that shapes how others consult, advise, and lead.

By writing a book, you preserve your frameworks, share your insights, and provide others—consultants, clients, and business leaders—with tools they can revisit again and again. You're not just creating a resource for the present; you're leaving behind a professional blueprint that can guide future generations.

Moreover, authoring a book enables you to make a meaningful contribution to your industry's ongoing development.

Whether it's strategy, leadership, operations, transformation, or change management, your ideas become part of the conversation that moves the consulting field forward. Your legacy is measured not only by the number of clients you've served, but also by the impact of your ideas and how long they continue to resonate.

A book ensures that these ideas are not lost over time but continue to influence how businesses evolve, how consultants work, and how value is delivered.

So, when you write your book, you're not just compiling knowledge—you're cementing your authority, sharing what matters most, and leaving behind something that endures—something future consultants will quote, clients will trust, and the industry will remember.

Key Takeaways:

- **Marketing and Branding:** A book can be a cornerstone of your consulting brand strategy, offering a compelling way to communicate your values, expertise, and the outcomes you help clients achieve.

- **Leveraging Your Book for Business Growth:** By sharing your insights and frameworks, you can attract new clients, collaborators, and opportunities aligned with your consulting philosophy.

- **Media and PR Opportunities:** Books generate significant media and PR potential, positioning you as a subject-matter expert for interviews, features, podcasts, and thought leadership columns.

- **Establishing Thought Leadership:** Writing a book solidifies your position as a thought leader within your domain—be it strategy, operations, change management, or innovation.

***

6
Writing the Right Book

"In order to succeed. We must first believe that we can."

———**Nikos Kazantzakis**

There is a unique kind of satisfaction that consultants understand better than most. It's that quiet, decisive moment when months of rigorous analysis, sleepless nights, endless whiteboarding sessions, and carefully calibrated recommendations finally bear fruit. You've sat in countless meetings, mediated conflicting stakeholder agendas, and navigated shifting business landscapes. And then, at last, the strategy you designed, the transformation plan you championed, the change you helped shepherd—it all comes to life. Processes improve. Teams align. Revenue grows. The breakthrough happens.

In those moments, you feel something more than professional success. You feel pride. Purpose. Validation that your ideas mattered, that your efforts contributed to something larger than a single engagement. Now, imagine distilling that entire journey—not just from one project, but from years of such moments—into a book. A living, breathing document that carries your voice, your frameworks, and your hard-earned lessons to an audience far beyond your immediate circle of influence.

Instead of handing over a final report to one client, you hand the world a book with your name on the cover. It is no longer just a fleeting deliverable. It is a permanent record of what you know and what you stand for. It represents the wisdom gained from the battles fought in client boardrooms and the quiet clarity that comes from reflecting on those battles later.

Writing a book is not merely a business strategy. It is a profoundly personal victory.

For many consultants, the professional world is a series of projects, deadlines, and deliverables. We live by timelines and KPIs. Our success is measured in client satisfaction scores, market share increases, and cost savings realized. And while those outcomes are important, they are, by nature, temporary. The next quarter brings new problems. The next client brings new expectations. What we accomplished yesterday is quickly overshadowed by what we must solve tomorrow. A book, however, stands apart from that cycle. It is not an ephemeral deliverable that will be filed away in a project archive. It is a legacy piece. Something that lasts. Something that reflects the essence of your professional identity and intellectual contribution.

Think about the quiet power in that. Most of what we build as consultants belongs to our clients. Our ideas reside within their organizations, shaping their decisions and driving their outcomes. But a book that belongs to you. It is your narrative, told in your voice, carrying your vision. No approvals needed. No executive summaries sanitized for stakeholders—just your unfiltered perspective. There is freedom in that. And fulfillment.

Fulfillment because writing a book forces you to step back from the day-to-day rush of problem-solving and ask yourself more profound questions: What do I truly believe about my work? What patterns have I seen repeat across industries and clients? What frameworks have I crafted through trial and error that others could benefit from? What kind of impact do I want to make, not just on individual organizations, but on the way people think about my industry as a whole?

These are questions we rarely have time to answer in the middle of project execution. They are questions of purpose. Of legacy.

When you answer them through your book, you create something far larger than a consulting deliverable. You create a body of work that reflects your professional journey—its struggles, its triumphs, and everything in between.

The emotional impact of holding your published book in your hands for the first time cannot be overstated. The weight of the pages, the texture of the cover, the sight of your name on the spine—it's a moment that stays with you. Because it represents more than the finished manuscript, it represents every late night you wrestled with doubt, every early morning you carved out time to write, every decision to persist when it would have been easier to postpone. It is tangible proof that you saw a creative journey through to completion.

In an industry where our work is often invisible—buried in internal portals, NDA-protected deliverables, and confidential boardroom discussions—a book makes your thinking visible. Accessible. Shareable.

It allows your ideas to travel beyond your immediate reach. Clients you've never met, aspiring consultants halfway around the world, students entering the profession—all of them can learn from your experiences. Your book becomes a lighthouse, guiding others through challenges you've already navigated. And in doing so, it amplifies your impact far beyond the scope of your projects.

Such a level of reach is rare in the consulting industry. Our influence, although meaningful, is typically limited to the scope of our client engagements. But a book creates leverage. It multiplies your voice. It allows your influence to extend into conversations, organizations, and industries you may never directly interact with.

And beyond all the professional benefits—beyond the speaking invitations, the expanded network, the new business leads—there is a quieter, more personal reward: pride.

Pride, not in the ego-driven sense of accomplishment, but in the more profound sense of having created something that matters. Something you can look back on and say, "This is what I've learned. This is what I believe. This is what I hope others will carry forward." Writing a book is also a journey of personal growth. Along the way, you confront your mental blocks: perfectionism, impostor syndrome, and fear of criticism. You wrestle with doubts about whether your ideas are "good enough" or "original enough."

And through that process, you come to realize that your value doesn't lie in having all the answers. It lies in your willingness to share what you've learned so far. Authorship is an act of generosity, not of ego.

And let's be honest—writing a book is hard. Much like leading a complex consulting engagement, it tests your discipline, your resilience, and your focus. There are moments when the words won't flow, when the structure feels tangled, when your confidence falters. But as with any challenging project, persistence pays off. And when you reach the final chapter, the final edit, the final approval from your publisher, you will find a sense of fulfillment that few professional milestones can match.

Unlike most career accomplishments, a book is something you've built on your terms. No client dictated the scope. No stakeholder controlled the narrative. This was your vision, executed your way.

In this way, writing a book mirrors the journey of any great consultant. You saw a problem—in this case, the underrepresentation of your voice in the broader professional conversation. You crafted a strategy—dedicated writing time, outlined your ideas, sought feedback, and refined your message. And you executed it, step by step, until the vision became a reality.

The joy of authorship is not just in holding the finished book; it's in the creative struggle that got you there. Much like the consulting process itself, it's in the clarity that emerges from iteration. The insights that surface from reflection. Breakthroughs occur when you push past resistance and keep moving forward.

And then there is the legacy. A book outlives a career. Long after you've moved on from active consulting, your ideas will continue to shape conversations. Future generations of consultants may cite your frameworks, build upon your methodologies, or challenge your assumptions. Your book becomes part of the intellectual fabric of your field.

Few career achievements offer that kind of enduring influence. Perhaps you didn't set out to leave a legacy. Many start simply wanting to share our story, our frameworks, our lessons. But legacy is what happens when you create something of lasting value. Something others can learn from, apply, and build upon.

And perhaps, years from now, someone you've never met will pick up your book in a university library, a co-working space, or a quiet airport lounge. And in reading your words, they'll find the clarity they need for their next big decision, their next bold move, their next chapter.

That is the power of authorship. And that is its ultimate fulfillment. It is easy, in the relentless pace of consulting, to lose sight of the bigger picture. To move from one project to the next without pausing to reflect on the journey so far, and writing a book forces that pause. It invites you to step back, take stock, and ask yourself what you've truly learned along the way.

By sharing that learning, you not only enrich your career but also enrich the careers of others.

So when you think about writing a book, please don't see it only as a professional milestone, though it certainly is one. See it as a creative act. A personal declaration. A lasting gift. And when the day comes that you place your finished book on your bookshelf—next to the industry greats you've long admired—you'll know that your voice now stands among them.

You'll know that you didn't just build a career; you've built a legacy. You contributed. And that is fulfillment worth pursuing.

Achieving Personal Milestones

Writing a book is a significant personal milestone. It's a concrete expression of your consulting expertise, your professional journey, and the dedication you've invested over the years. Completing a book takes discipline, clarity of thought, and a strong commitment to your subject.

The path from concept to published manuscript is rarely straightforward—it's often long, demanding, and full of learning curves. But the moment you hold your book in your hands, the sense of fulfillment is unparalleled. Writing a book is as much a journey of personal growth and self-reflection as it is a professional endeavor. When you stay focused on your purpose—on the difference your insights might make—you'll find the process incredibly rewarding.

Just imagine it: someone out there is seeking answers to a challenge, professionally or personally, and your book becomes the guide they didn't know they needed.

The Personal Satisfaction of Becoming a Published Author

Writing a book is a deeply transformative journey. It challenges you to pause, reflect on your consulting experiences, organize your insights, and express your professional vision with clarity and purpose. This process of reflection isn't just intellectually rewarding—it helps you deepen your understanding of your methods, values, and expertise.

For many consultants, becoming a published author is a milestone that brings immense personal satisfaction. It's similar to completing a complex engagement or leading a client through a significant breakthrough. Becoming a published author is a testament to your persistence, discipline, and the depth of your thinking. Moreover, it affirms your confidence in your knowledge and reinforces your professional identity.

Example: David A. Fields and The Irresistible Consultant's Guide to Winning Clients

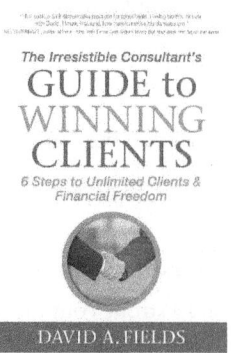

David A. Fields, a seasoned consultant and coach to consulting firms, authored *The Irresistible Consultant's Guide to Winning Clients* to share his frameworks for client acquisition. The act of writing the book allowed him to consolidate years of experience into a clear, teachable system. It not only elevated his visibility in the consulting world but also brought a deep sense of fulfillment, knowing his approach was now helping consultants across the globe win more business with confidence. For Fields, the personal reward wasn't just in the business growth, but in seeing his knowledge create real impact beyond his immediate circle.

Sharing Your Journey and Experiences

Writing a book gives you a powerful platform to share your consulting journey and the insights you've gathered along the way. Your story—complete with wins, missteps, lessons, and breakthroughs—can educate, inspire, and empower others who are navigating similar paths in their professional lives.

By being open about the challenges you've faced and the strategies you've developed to overcome them, you offer valuable, real-world guidance to your readers. For fellow consultants, aspiring professionals, or even clients, your book becomes more than a collection of ideas—it becomes a trusted resource and a source of encouragement. When you put your experiences into words, you're not just telling your story—you're creating a lasting impact.

The Impact of Sharing Your Story

Sharing your story through a book can create a meaningful impact on your readers. It doesn't just inform—it inspires, empowers, and provides actionable insights. When you document your consulting journey, including the challenges, lessons, and philosophies you've learned, your book becomes a trusted guide for others navigating a similar path. For many readers, it can be the very push they need to navigate uncertainty, refine their thinking, or elevate their consulting practice.

This sense of contribution—of knowing your story is making a difference—is deeply fulfilling. And the genuine feedback you receive from readers whose careers and confidence have grown because of your book is one of the most rewarding aspects of becoming an author.

Leaving a Legacy

Some consultants might say, "I'm not writing for fame or recognition—I just want to document my journey, for myself or for those who come after me." And that's not only valid, but also deeply meaningful. Many professionals go through decades of hard-earned experiences, face unique challenges, and gather insights that are too valuable to remain undocumented.

Writing a book becomes a way to preserve that wisdom, not for sales or status, but to ensure that your ideas, your learnings, and your story live on. You may have discovered strategies, frameworks, or truths that someone out there desperately needs, but no one else is offering them quite the way you can. At Stardom Books, we've seen consultants and seasoned professionals write books purely for this reason—to create something lasting, something that outlives them. Some choose to write part memoir, part guidebook, weaving together personal stories, client experiences, and the lessons they've distilled over time.

A book allows you to leave behind more than just a résumé or a list of clients—it becomes a permanent record of your thinking, your contributions, and your voice. For future generations of consultants, professionals, and even your own family, your book can become a lasting source of learning, inspiration, and enduring impact, long after your projects are complete and your practice has come to an end.

Creating a Lasting Impact in Your Field

Writing a book enables you to make a meaningful contribution to the body of knowledge within your field. Your insights, drawn from hands-on experience and real client work, can offer valuable additions to the ongoing discourse in your industry. By sharing your expertise, you don't just inform—you help shape the future of your profession and leave a lasting mark. A book also allows you to create a legacy that extends far beyond your immediate role or firm. It becomes a tangible record of your thinking and contribution—something that can inform, guide, and inspire future generations. Your work can serve as a beacon for others, illuminating the path and providing a reference point for those seeking to grow and evolve in the consulting world.

Writing a book as a consultant is a powerful opportunity to influence your industry, accelerate your growth, and leave a lasting legacy that continues to make a difference long after your engagements have ended.

Contributing to Consulting Literature and Education

Beginning the journey of writing a book is embarking on a transformative intellectual adventure. It's an invitation to explore your depth of thinking, articulate your ideas with creativity and clarity, and connect with readers in a lasting, impactful way. By embracing the discipline, focus, and dedication required, consultants can join the ranks of professionals who've left an indelible mark on industry literature and the broader professional community.

Your book can become a valuable addition to the consulting knowledge base, providing meaningful resources for aspiring consultants, educators, and clients alike. By sharing your expertise and real-world experiences, you contribute to the education of the next generation of consultants and play a crucial role in shaping the industry's future.

Example: Patrick Lencioni and The Five Dysfunctions of a Team

Patrick Lencioni, a respected business consultant and founder of The Table Group, authored *The Five Dysfunctions of a Team* to address common organizational challenges through a unique blend of storytelling and practical insight. His book, widely adopted in leadership training and MBA programs, has become a foundational text for consultants working in organizational health, leadership development, and team dynamics. Lencioni's work continues to influence how consultants diagnose team issues and advise clients, making his contribution to consulting literature both impactful and enduring.

Personal and Professional Growth

As seen in the examples shared throughout this book, these works are more than just printed pages—they've become vehicles for deep personal growth and amplified influence.

For consultants who chose to author them, these books not only built thought leadership but helped shape personal brands that extend far beyond boardrooms and client meetings. Their ideas have sparked conversations, challenged conventional thinking, and driven real change, blending the worlds of consulting insight and professional literature into something transformative.

Writing a book catalyzes both personal and professional growth. The process of researching, writing, and eventually promoting your book pushes you to refine your thinking, expand your skill set, and articulate your expertise more effectively. This growth often leads to new perspectives, sharper communication, and greater confidence in your consulting practice.

The journey of writing is not simply about organizing knowledge—it's about transformation through knowledge. Authors are required to delve deeply into their subject, engage in research and self-inquiry, and revisit their professional experiences through a fresh lens. This process fosters clarity, self-awareness, and a more holistic understanding of your field, making you not just a better consultant but a more evolved professional.

The Development of New Skills

The process of writing a book requires a diverse set of skills, including research, writing, editing, communication, and marketing. By committing to this journey, consultants have the opportunity to develop and sharpen these capabilities, strengthening their overall professional toolkit.

These new or refined skills don't just support the book project—they become invaluable assets in your consulting work, enabling you to take on new challenges and seize fresh opportunities.

Completing a book is not just about crossing a finish line—it's the culmination of focused effort, strategic thinking, and long-term dedication. Publishing a book fosters a deep sense of achievement, reinforcing your confidence and validating your expertise in a tangible, public way. As readers engage with your work and recognize the value in your insights, the feedback and appreciation you receive affirm your authority in your field.

This recognition—whether from peers, clients, or industry leaders—strengthens your self-assurance and empowers you to present your ideas with clarity and conviction.

While immensely rewarding, the writing journey is rarely without obstacles. From navigating writer's block to handling critique, the process demands resilience. Overcoming these challenges reinforces your belief in your ability to persist through adversity, further bolstering your confidence not just as a writer but as a professional.

Example: David Maister and Managing the Professional Service Firm

David Maister, a former Harvard Business School professor and consultant to professional service firms, authored *Managing the Professional Service Firm* after years of advising consulting, legal, and accounting firms. Although he came from an academic background, the writing and publishing process required him to translate complex industry insights into accessible and actionable ideas. Through this journey, Maister not only honed his skills in communication and thought leadership but also elevated his profile globally. His book became a cornerstone text in the consulting world, opening doors to new engagements and further solidifying his influence across the industry.

Expanding Your Knowledge and Expertise

Writing a book requires extensive research and deep reflection on your professional experiences and accumulated insights. This process naturally expands your knowledge and sharpens your expertise, offering you a more nuanced and holistic understanding of your consulting domain.

Authors are often pushed to examine their work more critically, dissecting projects, lessons, and methodologies in search of valuable insights. This act of reflection encourages consultants to look at their journeys from multiple angles, often revealing layers of meaning or connections that were previously overlooked. As you organize your expertise into a structured narrative, patterns begin to emerge. Seemingly unrelated client experiences or frameworks start to connect, enriching your perspective and revealing more profound truths about your practice. This interlinking of ideas doesn't just improve your book—it transforms the way you think and consult.

Example: Ram Charan and Execution: The Discipline of Getting Things Done

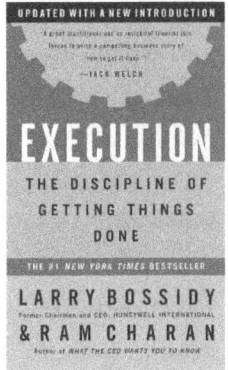

Ram Charan, a renowned business consultant and advisor to Fortune 500 CEOs, co-authored *Execution: The Discipline of Getting Things Done* with Larry Bossidy. The process of writing the book required Charan to draw from decades of client engagements and distill his principles into a clear, actionable framework. In doing so, he revisited and re-examined the underlying logic behind his most successful strategies. This exercise not only deepened his understanding of execution and leadership but also strengthened his reputation as a global authority in business consulting. The book went on to become a bestseller, opening up further teaching opportunities, advising, and thought leadership.

Creating New Opportunities

Writing and promoting a book can open doors to new and exciting opportunities for growth and advancement in your consulting career. By positioning yourself as an expert and thought leader, your book becomes a magnet for potential speaking engagements, consulting projects, and strategic collaborations. A book's reach extends far beyond its immediate audience—it attracts professionals, industry leaders, decision-makers, and even media attention. For consultants, publishing a book often acts as a catalyst for expanding their network, forging relationships across industries and geographies, and building influence within their professional ecosystem.

Your book can spark meaningful transformation in your career. It has the potential to shift the trajectory of your professional path, creating new avenues for collaboration, teaching, or even a full-time writing and advisory role. The impact of authorship frequently extends beyond the content itself, helping you redefine what's possible in your consulting journey.

Building a Personal Brand

Writing a book can play a pivotal role in helping you craft and strengthen a compelling personal brand. It enhances your visibility, credibility, and authority within your niche. A well-written book showcases not only your expertise but also your unique perspective and approach, allowing you to stand out in the crowded consulting landscape. Your book becomes a foundational tool in amplifying your brand. It positions you as a trusted expert and gives readers a sense of your voice, values, and professional philosophy. These elements are central to personal branding, and a book offers a platform to express them consistently and impactfully.

Use your book to clearly articulate your experience in a particular domain through case studies, frameworks, stories, and strategic insights. This substantiates your expertise and builds trust with your audience. That trust is essential in consulting, where personal credibility often drives client decisions.

It's equally important to develop a writing style that reflects authenticity and distinctiveness. When your book feels like an honest expression of who you are and how you think, it naturally sets you apart. This personal touch not only inspires readers but also helps them connect with you on a deeper level.

Extend your brand identity throughout the book's design, tone, and structure. Ensure it reflects your consulting ethos, values, and aesthetic. A well-aligned book reinforces your brand image, fosters recognition, and instills confidence in your readers about your expertise and approach.

The Significance of a Personal Brand

A strong personal brand can set you apart in the consulting world, making you more recognizable, respected, and sought after. It strengthens your credibility and extends your influence, leading to new opportunities and meaningful professional connections. A book serves as a powerful tool to establish and reinforce that brand.

Publishing a book allows you to introduce original ideas, challenge conventional thinking, and shape conversations within your industry. It positions you as a thought leader—someone who not only understands the current landscape but helps define its future. In the world of consulting, where expertise and perspective are your core offerings, this visibility is invaluable.

Thought leaders use books to spark change. Through clear arguments, compelling frameworks, and future-focused strategies, your book can reflect your vision and establish your voice as a driving force in your niche. It signals to clients, peers, and industry stakeholders that your insights are not only relevant but influential.

Your book also gives readers a window into your journey—your challenges, breakthroughs, and lessons learned. That human element makes you more relatable and trustworthy, especially in a relationship-driven field like consulting. People connect not just with your ideas, but also with your story.

Ultimately, your book becomes a strategic asset. It boosts your leadership presence, opens doors to new networks, accelerates your career growth, and creates a lasting impact. It contributes to your industry's body of knowledge while enhancing your brand in ways that extend well beyond the page.

Inspiring and Empowering others

Writing a book gives you a powerful opportunity to inspire and empower others by sharing your knowledge, experiences, and insights. As a consultant, your journey is filled with lessons—hard-earned strategies, tested frameworks, and moments of growth—that can offer meaningful guidance to others navigating similar paths.

Your book can serve as a beacon for emerging consultants, professionals transitioning into advisory roles, or even corporate leaders seeking clarity in uncertain times. By candidly sharing your challenges and the solutions you've discovered, you demonstrate to others what's possible—and how to achieve it.

In doing so, you not only position yourself as an expert but also as a mentor-at-scale. Your words can help others overcome their roadblocks, spark new thinking, and push past doubts. A book enables you to extend your impact far beyond your immediate clients, reaching people who may never meet you in person—but who benefit from your wisdom just the same.

Whether it's through a case study, a personal story, or a powerful idea, your book can be a source of motivation, resilience, and direction. For many readers, especially those in consulting or business leadership, your insights could be the encouragement they need to take their next bold step.

Creating a Sense of Fulfillment

Ultimately, writing a book offers a deep sense of fulfillment—it allows you to reach a meaningful personal and professional milestone. For consultants, it's more than just putting thoughts on paper; it's about contributing something lasting and valuable to your field. The act of distilling your knowledge, sharing your experiences, and knowing that your work can influence and guide others brings profound satisfaction. Whether you're helping a new consultant find their footing, offering clarity to a business leader, or simply telling your own story, your book becomes a powerful tool for impact.

There's immense joy in knowing that your expertise lives beyond the confines of a single project or client. You're creating something enduring—something that reflects your values, your voice, and your unique approach to solving problems. Such a legacy offers both pride and purpose.

Publishing a book is a moment of reflection and reward—a culmination of years of learning and doing. The fulfillment comes not only from what the book does for others but also from what it represents in their journey: growth, contribution, and lasting influence.

Key Takeaways:

- **Sharing Your Journey and Expertise:** Publishing a book enables you to share your consulting journey and hard-earned insights with a broader audience, offering valuable lessons, inspiration, and practical guidance.

- **Leaving a Legacy:** A book preserves your unique knowledge and perspectives, creating a lasting legacy that continues to educate and inspire others long after your projects end.

- **Creating New Opportunities:** Publishing a book can open doors to new career paths, consulting engagements, collaborations, teaching roles, and speaking invitations, thereby elevating your visibility and impact.

- **Creating a Sense of Fulfillment:** Knowing that your book is making a positive difference and leaving a meaningful impact offers a unique and lasting sense of fulfillment, both personally and professionally.

***

7

How & Where To Get Professional Help

"Mentoring is a brain to pick, an ear to listen, and a push in the right direction."

Why Consultants Should Hire A Publishing Coach

For consultants, few professional endeavors feel as personal and as public as writing a book. It's a project that extends beyond mere knowledge sharing. It becomes a representation of your leadership, your thinking, and your vision. And yet, despite the years of clarity, confidence, and strategic discipline you bring to your client work, the journey of writing a book can feel surprisingly overwhelming.

The blank page, the endless drafts, the uncertainty over structure, tone, and market fit, all of it can stall your momentum before the first chapter is complete.

That's where the right publishing coach becomes invaluable. Not as a ghostwriter who takes the work off your hands, nor as a passive editor who checks for grammatical accuracy, but as a strategic partner who helps you bring clarity, momentum, and market alignment to your authorship journey. In many ways, working with a publishing coach mirrors the consulting relationship itself.

Just as your clients rely on you to navigate complexity, identify blind spots, and accelerate outcomes, you, as an author, benefit from a trusted advisor who sees the entire publishing landscape more clearly than you do from inside your process.

When you engage a publishing coach, you're making a strategic investment not just in completing your manuscript but in ensuring the final book aligns with your broader business goals and brand narrative. The book is not simply a creative endeavor—it is a business asset. And like any valuable business asset, it requires intentional design, rigorous execution, and strategic deployment. A publishing coach begins by helping you create a clear roadmap for your project. In the consulting world, no major transformation happens without a plan. The same applies to your book. Without a roadmap, the process becomes reactive, driven by bursts of inspiration or fits of frustration. You might write a chapter here, draft an outline there, rewrite the introduction six times, and still feel no closer to completion.

A coach changes that dynamic. They help you break down the enormous task of "writing a book" into manageable phases with achievable milestones. Maybe the first month is dedicated solely to sharpening your book concept and audience positioning. Perhaps the next phase focuses on outlining the chapters and mapping your intellectual property into a cohesive narrative arc. Then comes the disciplined writing sprints, each one designed to build momentum rather than perfection.

When inevitable obstacles appear, such as writer's block, doubt, or competing work priorities, a coach offers not only encouragement but also practical course corrections. They remind you why this project matters. They help you pivot your approach without losing sight of the goal. They hold you accountable in the way your best consulting engagements hold leadership teams accountable to their transformation goals.

But their role extends beyond merely keeping you on track. A skilled publishing coach helps you shape your book's positioning. They ask the questions you may not have thought to ask yourself: How does this book reflect your consulting brand? What differentiates your approach from the dozens of other books on your topic? How will your target audience benefit from this book, and what action do you want them to take after reading it?

These aren't theoretical questions. They serve as strategic guardrails, ensuring your book is not just an exercise in personal expression but a catalyst for professional growth.

Because let's face it: as a consultant, your time is precious. You're not writing this book to tell your story. You're writing it to build your thought leadership platform, attract the right clients, open doors to speaking engagements, and expand your market influence. Every chapter, every anecdote, every framework should serve those larger goals. A publishing coach ensures that it happens.

They also help streamline the writing process itself. Many first-time authors struggle to find their writing rhythm. Should you write in the mornings, carve out full-day writing retreats, or chip away at the manuscript during lunch breaks? Should you write linearly from chapter one to the conclusion, or tackle the sections where you feel most inspired first? How do you balance storytelling with practical frameworks, or personal voice with professional tone?

A coach doesn't hand you a one-size-fits-all formula. Instead, they help you discover a process that fits your lifestyle, your personality, and your work rhythms. They help you balance your consulting commitments with your writing milestones, ensuring steady progress rather than sporadic progress. And the journey doesn't end with a finished manuscript. A book without readers is simply a personal journal. The actual value of your book is unlocked in how it's positioned, published, and promoted. A coach helps you think through your author platform—how your book fits into your existing digital presence, your speaking engagements, your LinkedIn strategy, your website, and your media outreach.

They help you map out your launch strategy, not just for day one of publication, but for the months that follow. Should you pursue media interviews, guest podcasts, and industry panels? Should you organize a book launch event, host a webinar series, or bundle the book with your consulting workshops? These are tactical choices, but they have strategic consequences for how your book drives business growth.

In this way, a publishing coach becomes more than a writing mentor. They become a trusted advisor for your author brand. They help you zoom out from the individual chapters and see the bigger picture: how your book fits into your career trajectory, your market positioning, and your long-term vision. Choosing the right coach, then, is a critical decision. Because not every coach understands the world of consulting. Some may focus on the literary craft, helping you refine your narrative voice, but lack the business acumen to align your book with your consulting practice. Others may offer generic publishing advice without tailoring it to your industry niche or your professional goals.

The right coach brings a blend of editorial insight and business strategy. They understand that your book is not an isolated creative project but a core part of your professional platform. They respect your consulting expertise and help translate it into accessible, engaging writing without diluting its depth.

They also understand the unique time pressures consultants face. You're not taking a six-month sabbatical to write this book. You're balancing it alongside client deliverables, business development efforts, and perhaps personal commitments. A coach who respects those realities will help you create a writing plan that fits your life, rather than disrupting it.

The relationship with your publishing coach should feel collaborative, not prescriptive. You're not handing over your voice to someone else. You're sharpening it. You're clarifying it. And in that process, your coach challenges you to dig deeper into your frameworks, your stories, your lessons learned—so that what emerges is a book that truly reflects the depth of your expertise.

And when the day comes that you hold your finished book in your hands, it won't feel like a solo achievement. It will feel like the product of a trusted partnership—one where your ideas, your experiences, and your aspirations were shaped, sharpened, and supported every step of the way. Beyond the tactical support, the best coaches also offer something subtler but equally valuable: belief. The belief that your voice matters. Your story is worth telling. That your ideas can shape conversations beyond your current network, this belief becomes your fuel on the days when doubt creeps in.

In the mornings when the words won't flow. In the evenings, when you wonder if the effort is worth it.

A coach holds space for your ambition and keeps you moving toward it. For many consultants, the act of writing a book is the first time they've put themselves, not just their recommendations, in the spotlight. In client engagements, your ideas are evaluated on their merit, but they are delivered within a safe context: a boardroom, a deliverable, a known relationship. A book is different. It is published for the world to read, critique, and engage with. That vulnerability can be daunting.

A coach helps you navigate that vulnerability with grace. They help you frame your message with confidence and humility. They remind you that your goal is not to be perfect, but to be useful. And in doing so, they free you from the paralysis of perfectionism that so often derails first-time authors. Ultimately, writing a book is a leadership act. You are leading a conversation in your field. You are creating a body of work that will outlive your current projects. And like any act of leadership, it's a journey best undertaken with trusted allies. A publishing coach is that ally.

They are your strategist, your editor, your accountability partner, and your cheerleader. They help you navigate the publishing landscape, avoid common pitfalls, and maximize the return on your time and intellectual investment. And just as your clients turn to you to lead them through transformation, you can turn to your coach to lead you through the transformation of authorship.

Because when your book is finally out in the world, shaping minds, sparking conversations, and opening doors, you'll look back and realize that the decision to work with a coach wasn't simply about writing a book. It was about building a legacy.

Values Alignment

Does the coach align with your personal and professional values? For instance, if you're a results-driven yet flexible consultant who thrives on creative freedom, and your coach operates like a rigid taskmaster, friction is inevitable.

You may find their style obstructive instead of empowering. Even subtle mismatches in values—such as how they perceive thought leadership, branding, or client relationships—can derail the process. A coach who understands your worldview will help you write in a voice that's authentically yours.

Verifiable Results

Has the coach walked the path you're on? Have they published books that made an impact in consulting, built thought leadership platforms, or grown authority-based businesses? Or do they "teach the theory" from the sidelines? You want someone who has not only mastered the mechanics of publishing but also used books to grow influence, attract clients, or secure speaking gigs. Look for someone who can show—not just tell—what success in this space looks like. Their journey should serve as proof that what they teach works.

Also, remember that success is relative. Choose a coach who embodies the kind of success *you* aspire to—whether that's prestige, profitability, or purpose-driven influence.

Experienced and Qualified

Publishing a book as a consultant isn't just about good grammar or layout—it's about positioning, messaging, and translating expertise into compelling content. So, is your coach truly equipped with the experience and education needed to help you succeed? Or are they simply repackaging surface-level insights from others?

Ideally, your coach should be well-rounded in all three areas:

- A reader who understands books and frameworks that resonate in the consulting world.

- A writer who has authored impactful work.

- A publisher who has helped other consultants bring their books to life.

This combination ensures they understand both the strategy *and* the execution, just like a great consultant does in their client work.

Satisfied Clients

Before hiring any coach, examine their track record. Who have they worked with? Are their clients consultants like you? Did those clients successfully publish, grow their authority, or generate leads through their books?

Testimonials, case studies, and reviews can offer valuable insight into the coach's effectiveness. Knowing that others in the consulting world have been guided well and are satisfied with the results will give you confidence that you're making a wise investment.

Program Content and Coaching Style

Is the process structured in a way that suits your style as a consultant?

Consultants are strategic thinkers, so ask whether the coach's process feels logical, tailored, and results-oriented. Does it support your expertise or try to reshape it into something inauthentic?

The book-writing process should be an extension of your consulting brand, not a detour from it. You'll be more engaged—and your final manuscript more impactful—if the methods feel aligned with your tone, voice, and values.

Handling Challenges Head-On

Consultants are problem-solvers, but every thought leader faces challenges on the path to publication. So ask: Has the coach navigated setbacks—either in publishing or in life?

A coach who has pushed through obstacles brings more than advice—they bring perspective. That resilience can help you face common publishing roadblocks with clarity and composure.

If they've "been where you are," you'll trust their advice even more when challenges arise.

Learning Structure and Progress Tracking

Just like any consulting engagement, a clear framework and review process are essential. Does the coach offer a defined structure, progress milestones, and measurable outcomes? Make sure you're not just being motivated—you should also be *advancing*.

After a few weeks or sessions, assess how the relationship is working for you. If the coaching doesn't support your goals or growth, don't hesitate to adjust course. A good coach will welcome open dialogue and adaptation.

Use these factors as a checklist. They'll help ensure you find a coach who understands the unique demands of consultants—and can guide you toward a book that elevates both your brand and your business.

Publishing Pathways For Consultants

In today's evolving publishing ecosystem, consultants seeking to author a book are no longer limited to a single path. Whether your goal is to showcase thought leadership, generate leads, build credibility, or share your methodology at scale, there's a publishing model to suit your intent and resources.

Understanding the options—and how they align with your brand, timeline, and ambitions—is essential. Here are the three primary publishing routes available today, each offering its mix of control, investment, and professional support:

- **Traditional Publishing: Authority Meets Establishment** – This is the classic route, where a publishing house selects your manuscript, funds the production process, and handles distribution.

Pros: Wide distribution, industry credibility, professional editing/design.

Cons: Highly competitive, slower timelines, limited creative control, and reduced royalties.

Traditional publishing can elevate the positioning of consultants with a significant public profile, media presence, or strong platform, but the gatekeeping process is intense.

- **Self-Publishing: Autonomy in Action** – Ideal for consultants who value speed, creative control, and ownership. Self-publishing allows you to call the shots—from cover design to pricing—while retaining most of the profits.

Pros: Faster to market, complete control, higher royalties.

The cons: You manage everything—editing, formatting, marketing, and distribution (unless you hire help).

This path can be incredibly empowering for action-oriented and entrepreneurial consultants, especially when paired with a well-planned launch strategy.

- **Hybrid Publishing: Strategy Meets Support** – A middle ground between the two. Hybrid publishers offer professional services—editing, design, distribution—while you retain more control and contribute to costs.

Pros: High-quality output, quicker timelines than traditional methods, and shared responsibility.

Cons: Requires investment, and quality can vary between hybrid publishers.

Hybrid publishing offers a compelling balance for consultants who want professional-grade support without relinquishing ownership or waiting years for approval.

Which Path Should You Take?

Your choice should depend on what you value most:

- If positioning and prestige are key, traditional may appeal.

- If speed and control matter more, self-publishing offers the fastest ROI.

- If you want support with flexibility, a hybrid could be your best fit.

Remember, as a consultant, your book is more than a product—it's a platform. Select a publishing path that not only brings your ideas to the world but also aligns with your business model, brand image, and growth objectives.

At Stardom Books, we champion a hybrid publishing model that blends professional expertise with the consultant author's unique voice and strategic intent. This approach transforms publishing into a true partnership—one that respects your authority, supports your vision, and ensures that your final product is polished and positioned for impact.

As a consultant, your book isn't just content—it's a strategic asset. That's why our hybrid publishing model is designed to balance your influence with our infrastructure, giving you the best of both worlds: autonomy and expert guidance.

How Hybrid Publishing Serves Consultant-Authors:

- **Creative Control** – Unlike traditional publishing, hybrid publishing allows you to retain your unique tone, structure, and message. You're not boxed into rigid formats—your methodology, stories, and frameworks remain intact and authentic.

- **Professional Support** – You gain access to a team of experienced editors, designers, and marketing professionals who enhance your work without overriding your voice. It's a collaborative refinement, not a takeover.

- **Focus on What Matters** – You focus on your thought leadership—writing and strategy—while we handle the operational aspects, including production, distribution, and promotion. This enables you to maintain momentum in your consulting business without burning out.

- **True Partnership Approach** – We see our authors as partners, not just clients. This often translates into higher royalty percentages and a more transparent working relationship compared to traditional publishing houses.

- **Respect for Your Voice** – Our editorial philosophy is to preserve your voice, not dilute it. Your expertise, personality, and perspective remain center stage, critical for consultants looking to build trust and credibility through their book.

- **Flexibility and Adaptability** – As the industry evolves, so do we. Hybrid publishing enables greater agility, whether it involves adapting to new marketing platforms, testing innovative formats, or responding to shifting audience needs.

- **Mentorship and Strategic Guidance** – Throughout your publishing journey, you'll receive hands-on mentorship that aligns with your professional goals, helping you make better decisions on everything from chapter structuring to book promotion strategy.

While hybrid publishing offers a compelling mix of creative freedom and professional support, it's essential to consider a few key factors before determining if it's the right fit for your consulting goals.

- **Upfront Financial Investment** – Unlike traditional publishing, where the publisher bears most costs, or self-publishing, where expenses vary widely, hybrid publishing requires an initial investment from the author. This cost covers editing, design, production, and marketing, ensuring your book meets the highest professional standards. Think of it as a strategic business investment: you're financing a product that will elevate your brand and open new doors.

- **Lower Brand Recognition (for now)** – Hybrid publishing doesn't yet have the widespread name recognition of legacy publishing houses. However, brand prestige is becoming less relevant as industry lines blur and more successful entrepreneurs choose alternative models. Today, the value lies not in a logo on your spine but in your message, execution, and distribution strategy.

- **Perceived Prestige vs. Real Impact** – Some still view traditional publishing as more prestigious. But that perception is shifting, especially in the consulting world. Consultants care about results, reach, and reputation, not just pedigree. Many bestselling authors today have launched through hybrid or self-publishing routes, proving that credibility now comes from the value delivered, not the logo on the back cover.

The Trade-off Worth Making

Yes, hybrid publishing involves investment. But in return, you maintain your voice, gain expert support, and retain higher royalties. It offers the best of both worlds—the polish of traditional publishing with the agility and control of self-publishing.

Still, not all hybrid publishers are created equal. That's why it's vital to do your homework:

- Look at their past titles.

- Speak to authors they've worked with.

- Understand their royalty structure and editorial process.

When you find the right hybrid publisher, you get more than a book—you gain a powerful business asset that reflects your vision and enhances your authority in the market.

Why Choose Hybrid Publishing with Stardom Books?

For consultants and professionals seeking the perfect balance between control and credibility, Stardom Books offers a hybrid publishing model that delivers the best of both worlds—creative freedom with professional polish.

At Stardom Books, authors deserve both strategic influence and expert support. That's why we empower you to make key decisions about your book, while our experienced team ensures it's executed at a professional standard.

Here's What Sets Stardom Books Apart

- **Creative Freedom with Expert Guidance** – You retain full ownership of your ideas, voice, and narrative structure. Whether you're building a business case, sharing a signature framework, or crafting a thought leadership manifesto, your message remains authentically yours, refined with the help of seasoned editors, designers, and strategists.

- **Strategic Flexibility** – Our hybrid model is highly adaptable to your personal and professional goals. Whether your priority is maximizing reach, securing higher royalties, establishing niche influence, or achieving long-term brand positioning, we help you navigate the publishing process in a way that aligns with your business strategy.

- **Professional Quality & Market Readiness** – Your book isn't just published—it's polished, positioned, and promoted. Our expert team ensures high production standards, strategic marketing, and packaging that gives your message the visibility it deserves. From cover to copy, your book reflects your excellence.

- **Results That Speak for Themselves** – Take, for example, Srini Rajam, whose hybrid publishing journey with Stardom Books amplified his message and expanded his authority across industries. It's a testament to what's possible when entrepreneurial drive meets publishing expertise.

- **Smart Investment, Greater Returns** – Hybrid publishing at Stardom Books requires a moderate financial investment, but the returns—both tangible and intangible—can be substantial. You gain higher royalty percentages, increased brand recognition, and a platform that generates leads, credibility, and influence.

A Holistic Approach

We don't just publish books—we build legacies. Our services include:

- Strategic planning

- Book development & ghostwriting (if needed)

- Editing & design

- Publishing & distribution

- Marketing & PR support

- Guidance on leveraging your book for consulting growth, media coverage, and thought leadership.

The Stardom Advantage

In a world of confusing publishing options, Stardom Books offers clarity, support, and results. Whether your goal is to establish authority, generate leads, or influence an industry, our hybrid publishing model provides the infrastructure of traditional publishing with the flexibility of self-publishing.

It's more than just a publishing process—it's a partnership designed to turn your ideas into impact and your story into a strategic asset.

If you're serious about publishing a book that elevates your consulting career, Stardom Books is your ideal partner.

At Stardom Books, we believe that publishing a book should be a strategic, streamlined experience—one that positions you for authority, visibility, and long-term success. Our end-to-end hybrid publishing model ensures you are supported at every step—from idea to international distribution.

Here's how we transform your ideas into a published asset that builds your brand and grows your influence:

- **Planning: Tactical & Thoughtful Book Outline Creation** – Before a single word is written, our experienced publishing advisors help you develop a crystal-clear, strategically structured outline. Like architects drafting blueprints, we map out the flow, structure, and core arguments of your book to avoid guesswork and ensure alignment with your goals. This planning phase lays the foundation for a powerful, coherent manuscript.

- **Writing: Professional Writing Support** – Whether you're writing it yourself or collaborating with our expert writers, we guide you through a proven content creation system. We use tested frameworks, tools, and techniques to bring out your voice and message. The result? A compelling manuscript that reflects your expertise, without the overwhelm or time drain.

- **Finishing: Comprehensive Editing & Formatting** – Once the draft is complete, our editorial team takes over with multiple rounds of editing, proofreading, and formatting. We transform your manuscript into a publication-ready product with high aesthetic and professional standards. Every paragraph is polished, and every page is designed to impress.

- **Publishing: Global Publishing & Distribution** – Your book is published in print and digital formats and distributed globally across major platforms, including Amazon, Flipkart, Barnes & Noble, Apple Books, Kobo, and more.

We handle the logistics so you can focus on what matters—sharing your message with the world.

- **Leveraging: Author Coaching & Consulting** – Publishing is only the beginning. We provide post-launch consulting and coaching to help you position your book for maximum visibility and business impact. Whether your goal is to generate leads, attract speaking engagements, or enhance your consulting brand, we help you turn your book into a high-ROI strategic asset.

At Stardom Books, our process is more than publishing—it's a career-building journey. We equip you with everything you need to make your book not just credible and beautiful, but also profitable, influential, and aligned with your long-term professional vision.

In the fast-evolving world of books and content, the journey from idea to published work can be overwhelming, especially for first-time authors or entrepreneurs who balance writing with a busy professional life. That's where publishing and writing coaches come in. These experts don't just offer support—they provide direction, structure, and momentum to drive results.

A publishing coach serves as a strategic partner, guiding you through every stage of the book publishing journey. From refining your ideas to structuring your chapters and polishing your prose, they ensure your manuscript not only gets finished but also meets the highest editorial and market standards. Their role extends far beyond advice—they are co-architects of your success.

On the other hand, a writing coach dives deep into the mechanics of the craft. Think of them as your editor-in-residence—focused on tone, voice, storytelling, grammar, and narrative flow. Their job is to help you find your rhythm, refine your message, and captivate your readers from the first sentence to the last.

Whether you're a newcomer to the world of writing or a seasoned professional looking to elevate your voice, working with a coach exponentially increases your chances of success.

Why? Because they understand both the creative and commercial sides of publishing. They're constantly attuned to industry shifts, reader preferences, and what makes a book truly stand out.

By collaborating with a coach, you gain access to decades of distilled experience—a shortcut to mastering what most people take years to figure out. They help you avoid costly mistakes, stay accountable to your vision, and bring your best work into the world.

In a crowded marketplace, your book needs more than just good content. It needs structure, clarity, precision, and purpose. A skilled coach provides the scaffolding and support to turn your raw ideas into a refined, market-ready product. From strengthening your manuscript to sharpening your storytelling, a coach can take you from writer to published author—and from good to unforgettable.

Hiring a coach isn't an expense—it's an investment in authority, clarity, and long-term impact. For aspiring writers and growth-minded professionals alike, it can be the key to transforming intention into achievement.

Creating a Structured Path to Authority

Becoming an influential voice in your industry doesn't happen by chance—it requires intention, clarity, and a proven framework. That's where the Authority Influencer Roadmap comes in.

Many highly skilled professionals—consultants, entrepreneurs, specialists, and thought leaders—dedicate years to honing their craft. Yet, despite their expertise, they often remain invisible, under-recognized, and undervalued in their space. Not because they lack talent, but because they lack a structured approach to visibility and influence.

Let's get straight to the point: recognition is not a reward for hard work alone—it's the result of strategic positioning.

The Authority Influencer Roadmap provides precisely what you need. It's a three-phase journey designed to elevate you from being overlooked to becoming a recognized authority in your niche.

The stages are:

1. Plan—This phase clarifies your message, defines your audience, and outlines your thought leadership blueprint. It builds the foundation for your influence.

2. Build – Develop your assets: your book, your content, your platform. Here, you convert expertise into tangible tools of authority.

3. Launch – Share your message with the world through strategic marketing, visibility campaigns, and intentional brand positioning.

By following this roadmap, you'll gain more than just visibility—you'll establish genuine authority, enhance your reputation, strengthen your brand, and unlock opportunities that were previously out of reach.

It's not about chasing fame. It's about being seen by the right people for the right reasons—and making the impact your expertise truly deserves.

How to Follow the Authority Influencer Roadmap

The journey to becoming an industry influencer isn't just about being good at what you do—it's about positioning yourself strategically. The Authority Influencer Roadmap helps you do just that, through three essential stages: Plan, Build, and Launch.

PLAN: Define Your Message and Audience

In the first phase, your goal is to lay the strategic foundation for your authority. This involves three key actions:

- Getting in the Game – Understand your current positioning and decide to step into the spotlight.

- Identifying Your Circle of Influence – Clearly define who your ideal audience is—clients, collaborators, or industry peers.

- Crafting Your Core Message – Develop a resonant message that aligns your expertise with the goals, pain points, and aspirations of your target audience.

This phase is all about clarity—knowing who you are, who you serve, and what you stand for.

BUILD: Develop Your Platform and Content Ecosystem

With clarity established, the second phase focuses on creation and visibility. Here's what you'll do:

- Design Your Influence Model – Outline the framework or methodology that captures your unique approach to problem-solving.

- Create High-Impact Content—Write, speak, and record content that reflects your core message in multiple formats, including articles, videos, social posts, webinars, and more.

- Repurpose Strategically – Learn how to turn one great idea into ten assets that serve different platforms.

- Build Your Audience – Start growing your email list, social presence, and inbound traffic with targeted assets that lead people back to your message.

This stage turns your message into a movement, equipping you with a system for consistent visibility and authority.

LAUNCH: Establish Authority Through Your Book

This final phase is where everything comes together, culminating in the creation and publication of your book.

Writing a book is not just a content strategy—it's a credibility accelerator. It demonstrates expertise, opens doors to speaking and media opportunities, and gives you a tool that directly connects you with your target audience.

Once your book is out in the world, your influence multiplies. Readers become leads, opportunities start to flow in, and your voice begins to shape conversations in your niche. This phase is about maximizing your impact and visibility, solidifying your role as a trusted authority. By progressing through these three phases—Plan, Build, Launch—you transform your expertise into real influence. It's a roadmap not just for writing a book but also for amplifying your voice and expanding your legacy.

The Authority Influencer Roadmap is a robust framework, but its value lies in understanding and executing each phase with purpose and intention. Many startup founders and professionals struggle with where to begin when it comes to writing a book. This structured, nine-step process provides clarity, direction, and momentum—explicitly tailored for first-time authors seeking to make an impact.

1. Define Your Purpose

Before writing a single word, get clear on why you want to write this book. Is it to establish thought leadership? Build your business? Inspire change? When your purpose aligns with your personal and professional goals, it becomes your guiding compass throughout the journey.

2. Identify Your Audience

Knowing who you are writing for is just as important as knowing what to say. Define your target reader and understand their pain points, dreams, and daily struggles. This insight ensures your content resonates, connects, and converts.

3. Establish Your Key Message

What's the one core idea you want your readers to walk away with? Whether it's your unique methodology, a solution to a specific challenge, or a new way of thinking, your book needs a clear central message that anchors the entire narrative.

4. Create a Content Map or Outline

Structure is strategy. Develop a high-level outline that breaks your message into chapters or themes. Think of this as your architectural blueprint.

At Stardom Books, our publishing advisors help authors craft detailed outlines that save time and enhance clarity from the start.

5. Write the First Draft

Start drafting your manuscript based on the outline. Don't worry about perfection here—focus on getting your ideas out. If writing feels overwhelming, a professional writer can turn your outline into a compelling first draft through guided interviews or collaborative sessions.

6. Revise and Refine

Once your draft is complete, shift gears to editing. Fill gaps, clarify language, improve transitions, and polish your storytelling. With a publishing partner like Stardom Books, an editorial team will handle comprehensive reviews to elevate your manuscript to professional standards.

7. Prepare for Publishing

At this stage, your manuscript goes through final editing, formatting, and design. You'll work on selecting a compelling title, creating a high-impact cover, and ensuring your layout is both reader-friendly and visually appealing. Simultaneously, you'll begin planning your book's launch and marketing strategy.

8. Publish and Distribute

With everything in place, it's time to hit "publish." Determine which route best aligns with your goals—traditional, self-publishing, or hybrid. Stardom Books, for example, offers a hybrid model that combines professional publishing support with the freedom and control of self-publishing. Your book is distributed across major retailers globally—in print, eBook, or audiobook formats.

9. Promote and Leverage Your Book

Writing your book is only half the journey—marketing is what unlocks real impact. Promote your book through speaking engagements, podcast appearances, social media campaigns, guest blogs, and PR opportunities. Furthermore, leverage it as a strategic asset to elevate your brand, attract clients, open doors to media, and expand your influence in the market.

By following this structured roadmap—explicitly designed for startup founders—you can eliminate the uncertainty that often comes with starting a book. Each step provides clarity, direction, and momentum, helping you stay aligned with your purpose, speak directly to your ideal audience, and communicate your key message effectively.

With the guidance of publishing professionals like the team at Stardom Books, you're not navigating this journey alone. You'll have expert support at every stage, from planning to publishing and promotion, ensuring a smooth and rewarding experience.

Remember, writing a book is more than a creative pursuit—it's a strategic move that allows you to share your insights, build your authority, and reach a broader audience. Embrace the structure, trust the process, and step into your role as a published author with confidence. The roadmap is here. The opportunity is yours.

Partnering with a hybrid publishing house like Stardom Books offers a wide range of benefits designed to ensure your success as an author. Here's what you gain:

- **A Clear, Success-Oriented Strategy:** We help you build a structured roadmap with clear milestones to keep your book project on track and aligned with your goals.

- **A Proven Methodology:** Our systematic approach guides you through the entire book-writing and publishing journey with clarity and confidence.

- **Ongoing Progress Reviews:** We assess your development at regular intervals, making strategic adjustments as needed to keep you moving forward.

- **Content Structuring and Enhancement:** Our team supports you in organizing, developing, and elevating your book or proposal to a professional standard.

- **Time-Saving Tools and Templates:** You'll receive actionable blueprints, resources, and frameworks that simplify the publishing process and accelerate your book launch.

- **Author Platform Development:** We help you expand your visibility and presence as an author across key media and industry channels.

- **Strategic Book Promotion:** You'll be guided in crafting a compelling and comprehensive promotional plan tailored to your target audience.

***

Bonus

Keeping Momentum Long After Publishing

"The launch of your book is not an ending, but a pivotal beginning—what you do next determines whether it remains a fleeting spark or ignites a lasting flame."

———**Raam Anand**

Congratulations! You've done what many consultants only dream about: you've taken your expertise, experience, and unique perspective and translated them into a published book. The long hours of brainstorming, writing, revising, and refining have finally paid off. Maybe your launch day was met with excitement, positive feedback from your network, supportive clients and peers, and perhaps even some press coverage or initial sales. But here's the truth no one tells you: the real work begins after the launch. For many first-time consultant-authors, a natural lull follows the excitement of publishing. After weeks or months of planning your book release, coordinating promotional efforts, organizing virtual or in-person launch events, and sending out dozens of LinkedIn posts or newsletters, you might find yourself wondering: what's next?

This is where the mindset shift happens. Publishing your book was never meant to be a one-time event; it's meant to be the launchpad for long-term opportunities, visibility, and business growth. For consultants, a book can be one of the most strategic assets in your toolkit—but only if you actively keep it working for you.

With the right actions and attitude, your book can open doors, spark conversations, and deepen your authority in your niche for years to come.

Let's explore how you can sustain momentum long after your book is published and integrate it seamlessly into your consulting practice.

For consultants, your book is not primarily a product you're selling to generate royalties—it's a credibility builder, a marketing engine, and a conversation starter. The sales you make through Amazon or bookstores are just one small part of its value. The bigger payoff comes when the book helps you:

- Get invited to industry panels and conferences.

- Open doors to high-ticket consulting engagements.

- Serve as a leave-behind after sales meetings.

- Act as an in-depth business card that positions you as a thought leader.

- From the foundation of workshops, keynote speeches, or online courses.

So, rather than focusing solely on sales numbers post-launch, focus on how many business conversations your book initiates. Measure its success by the new relationships, collaborations, and speaking engagements it helps you secure.

The ideas in your book shouldn't stay trapped between its covers. Extract key insights, quotes, and frameworks and repurpose them into:

- LinkedIn articles and posts

- Blog series on your website

- Short-form videos sharing tips or case studies

- Podcast guest appearances or your podcast episodes

- White Papers or downloadable resources

Consistency is key. Schedule regular content that keeps your book—and by extension, your expertise—front of mind for your network.

People rarely buy a book the first time they hear about it; they buy when they keep hearing about it in ways that feel fresh, relevant, and valuable.

Consultants thrive on face-to-face influence—whether that's in the boardroom, at an industry conference, or during a webinar. Your book provides event organizers and decision-makers with a compelling reason to invite you to s eak. It shows them that you've organized your ideas into a coherent, valuable message.

Reach out to:

- Industry conferences relevant to your field.

- Corporate learning and development teams who may want internal training based on your book.

- Business associations and networking groups.

- Online summits and webinars.

Position yourself not just as an author, but as a speaker with a signature message drawn from your book—one that addresses the challenges your target audience faces.

Don't leave your book floating in isolation. Build it into your broader business strategy. Some ideas:

- Offer it as a gift when someone signs up for your newsletter or consulting discovery call.

- Send signed copies to prospective clients as part of a welcome kit or follow-up package.

- Use chapters from your book as gated content on your website.

- Create a companion workbook, guide, or template package as an upsell.

A book alone builds authority; when it's part of a broader client journey, it becomes a powerful business driver.

It's easy to think, "I posted about my book during the launch; everyone already knows." But in reality, most people won't see your first (or fifth) announcement. Keep sharing stories:

- Share reader testimonials and client success stories that relate to the themes of your book.

- Talk about how a chapter helped solve a real-world client problem.

- Reflect on what you've learned since writing the book and how your thinking has evolved.

This isn't repetitive—it's relationship-building. Every time you mention your book in a meaningful way, it reinforces your role as a trusted advisor in your space.

Your book launch is likely to have generated a burst of media interest, but don't let that be the end. Months (or even years) later, you can still pitch:

- Thought leadership articles in industry publications.

- Commentary opportunities on current events related to your book's topic.

- Interviews on podcasts, radio, or niche YouTube channels.

Position your book not as a time-sensitive release, but as a timeless resource that provides solutions to ongoing challenges in your industry.

If your industry evolves quickly or your frameworks mature, don't hesitate to plan a second edition or a follow-up product:

- A workbook version of your book.

- An online course expanding on its concepts.

- A new edition reflecting industry changes or new case studies.

This keeps your intellectual property fresh and relevant while giving your audience more ways to engage with your ideas.

Lastly, remember that consulting is a relationship business, and relationships take time. Your book is a powerful seed, but it's your consistent actions, generous sharing of expertise, and thoughtful follow-up that will help it bear fruit over time. Don't be discouraged if you don't see a flood of new clients immediately. Think of your book as a long-term investment in your brand and business, one that pays dividends when you stay engaged, visible, and helpful in your community.

Reframing The Post-launch Mindset For Consultants
1. Launch Day Is a Milestone, Not the Finish Line

For many consultants, writing and publishing a book feels like conquering a monumental personal and professional goal. The countless hours spent outlining chapters, polishing drafts, working with editors, and managing design and publishing logistics finally culminate in that moment when your book goes live. It's tempting to view this as the ultimate finish line—the peak of the journey.

But in reality, launch day is just the beginning.

While you absolutely should celebrate your accomplishment, it's essential to understand that the business impact of your book unfolds gradually, and almost entirely after publication. The launch builds initial awareness, but the most meaningful outcomes (new consulting engagements, media visibility, speaking invitations, and stronger client trust) emerge from sustained effort and visibility over time.

As a consultant, the power of your book lies in how you continue to leverage it strategically. Shifting your mindset from "I did it!" to "Now, how do I use this book as a catalyst for the next phase of my consulting practice?" is key to maintaining your momentum.

Why This Mindset Shift Matters for Consultants
- Steady Visibility Builds Authority: Books rarely create overnight thought leaders unless they are paired with ongoing marketing efforts. Whether you are active on LinkedIn, speaking at industry events, or publishing articles, your book should regularly reappear in conversations to keep your voice and expertise visible in your niche.

- Relationship-Building Over Time: Your most valuable opportunities—such as new clients, collaborations, media features, and introductions to decision-makers—often arise not during the launch week, but in the months that follow. These relationships deepen as your book continues to circulate within professional circles and is shared organically through word of mouth.

- Strategic Business Integration: The insights and frameworks you outlined in your book can fuel future consulting services, training programs, workshops, and brand messaging. However, this evolution occurs only if you actively engage with your content post-launch, reflect on its reception, and refine how you present your expertise.

Rather than seeing your book as a one-time achievement, embrace it as a dynamic asset that evolves alongside your consulting brand.

2. The "Slow Burn" Approach to Book Success

In today's fast-paced world, it's easy to fall into the trap of chasing instant gratification. You might hope your book will skyrocket to the bestseller list overnight, drive a flood of consulting inquiries, or earn immediate media coverage. However, sustainable success rarely occurs in this manner, especially in consulting, where trust and credibility are built gradually.

Instead, think of your book's journey as a slow burn. This approach acknowledges that lasting impact is the result of consistent, cumulative actions.

Your book may not trend on launch day, but over the weeks and months that follow, through speaking engagements, blog posts, client conversations, and social sharing, it can steadily establish your place as an authority in your s ace.

Elements of a Slow Burn Strategy:

- Word-of-Mouth Momentum: Some of the best referrals come from readers who found your helpful book long after its release. Encourage your clients, colleagues, and followers to recommend it to others in their professional and personal networks.

- Multiple Promotional Waves: Don't limit your marketing efforts to your launch week. Plan quarterly campaigns or thematic content releases that tie your book's message to relevant industry trends or seasonal conversations.

- Refining Your Messaging: The process of promoting your book teaches you what resonates with your audience. As you engage in podcast interviews, webinars, and consulting discussions, you'll gain clarity on which parts of your book spark the most interest. Use that feedback to sharpen your future marketing, talks, and services.

- Consistent Engagement: Your book's success thrives on your sustained visibility. Regular LinkedIn posts, newsletter insights, and speaking opportunities all help keep your message alive and evolving.

The Payoff of a Long-Term Mindset

Consultants who adopt this slow-burn perspective often experience deeper audience loyalty, higher-quality leads, and richer, more meaningful conversations. Instead of chasing short-lived metrics like launch-week downloads or Amazon rankings, they focus on building a lasting professional legacy.

Consider how your book fits into your broader consulting journey:
- What doors can it help you open over the next six months?

- How can you use it to educate your industry or raise awareness about critical challenges?

- What new products or services could you develop from its content?

Rather than measuring success by your launch day results, measure it by the meaningful interactions, business growth, and credibility you build steadily over time.

3. Practical Ways Consultants Can Sustain Post-Launch Momentum

If you're wondering how exactly to sustain this momentum after the initial excitement fades, here are some practical strategies designed for consultants:

- Include Your Book in Sales Conversations: Send prospective clients a copy of your book as part of your proposal follow-up or introductory conversation. It reinforces your authority and leaves a lasting impression.

- Offer Workshops Based on the Book: Many consultants turn their book into a training session, keynote talk, or leadership workshop for corporate clients. This creates additional revenue streams and positions you as both a thought leader and a practical problem solver.

- Build Content Pipelines: Don't let the writing end with your book. Extract key lessons from each chapter and transform them into LinkedIn posts, YouTube videos, or articles for industry magazines.

- Use Speaking Opportunities to Share Book Insights: When you speak at conferences, webinars, or on podcasts, be sure to mention your book. Not as a sales pitch, but as a source of deeper insights your audience can explore.

- Celebrate Reader Feedback: Encourage your audience to share how your book helped them. Highlight testimonials and success stories to keep building social proof.

Continuing To Promote Your Book Strategically

Publishing your book is an essential milestone in your consulting career, but maintaining its relevance requires strategic, ongoing effort. Your book should serve you well long after the excitement of the launch has faded. This means lanning continuous promotional activities and seamlessly integrating the book into your broader consulting ecosystem. Let's explore how to keep your book actively supporting your brand, your thought leadership, and your business growth.

1. Plan Promotional Waves, Not Just a One-Time Launch

A common misconception among first-time consultant-authors is that book promotion should only happen during the launch window. In truth, competent consultants treat their book like a product or service with periodic promotional bursts—or "mini-launches"—spread throughout the year. These campaigns help keep your book in front of your audience, especially as your consulting practice evolves or market trends shift.

Practical Ideas for Mini-Launches:

- Anniversary Campaigns: Celebrate your book's 6-month or 1st anniversary by offering a limited-time discount on the ebook or audiobook versions. Share behind-the-scenes stories of the writing journey, client wins tied to your book's concepts, or lessons learned since publication.

- Holiday or Awareness Month Tie-Ins: If your consulting focus aligns with specific calendar events (e.g., Leadership Month, Small Business Week, Mental Health Awareness), frame your book as a relevant resource. Offer it as a professional gift during the holidays or as recommended reading for industry professionals during themed months.

- Updated Editions or Bonus Content: Keep your book fresh by releasing a new edition with updated statistics, fresh case studies, or an exclusive foreword from a respected industry leader. This refresh gives you a great reason to promote the book again while positioning yourself as someone who evolves with your industry.

These periodic promotions aren't repetitive; they are reminders to your audience that your book remains timely and essential.

2. Tap into Ongoing Media and Publicity Opportunities

Don't stop your media efforts after the launch buzz settles. The reality is that media outlets, podcasts, and event organizers need fresh perspectives year-round. Your book equips you with an authoritative point of view—keep using it to stay part of the conversation.

Strategies for Sustained Visibility:

- Long-Tail Media Outreach: Industry magazines, business journals, and podcasts consistently seek timely commentary and insights. If your book's topic suddenly becomes newsworthy—say, due to regulatory changes or market shifts—reach out to offer your insights. Position yourself as someone who wrote about these issues before they became headlines.

- Recurring Columns and Articles: Seek opportunities to write a regular column in an industry publication or business blog where you can weave in insights from your book. Over time, these columns build both your brand and sustained interest in your book.

- Podcast and Webinar Appearances: Continue appearing on podcasts and webinars, even after the initial launch season. New shows emerge all the time, and your network of hosts from your pre-launch promotion may invite you back to discuss how your idea have evolved.

- Conference Speaking: If you missed out on speaking engagements during your launch phase, don't worry—conference schedules are constantly cycling. Submit speaking proposals, citing your book's impact, audience reviews, and your expertise. Event organizers are often seeking authors who have demonstrated staying power and a real-world application of their ideas.

By staying active in these channels, you reinforce your position as an industry thought leader, not just an author.

3. Integrate Your Book Into Your Consulting Business Ecosystem

Your book shouldn't sit on a shelf (physical or virtual); it should be an integral part of your consulting offers, lead generation strategy, and client onboarding process. Here are several ways to make your book work harder for you:

a. As a Lead Magnet or Client Touchpoint:

- Free or Discounted Copies as Incentives: Use your book as a value-added service. Offer a complimentary ebook when someone registers for your paid webinar, masterclass, or consulting session. You're not just giving away a book—you're establishing credibility before the first conversation even happens.

- Onboarding Gift for New Clients: Send signed copies of your book to new clients, especially those engaging you for long-term or high-ticket consulting projects. This thoughtful touch enhances your brand and sets a tone of value and thought leadership from the outset.

- Bundled With Existing Services: Consider bundling your book with a training session, workshop, or executive coaching engagement to enhance its value. This creates a more comprehensive learning experience for your clients.

b. Repurpose Your Book's Content Across Platforms:

A book isn't just one piece of content; it's a treasure trove of ideas. Break it down into smaller pieces to reach broader audiences:

- Blog Series: Turn each chapter (or key sections within them) into standalone blog posts. Expand on the core message, add real-world updates, or apply the framework to current trends. Always include a call to action that invites readers to explore the entire book.

- Video and Podcast Snippets: Record short video clips or audio segments where you explain key frameworks, client stories, or actionable tips from your book. Post these on LinkedIn, YouTube, Instagram, or even your email newsletter. These micro-content pieces pique curiosity and help new audiences discover your work.

- Email Drip Campaigns: Turn your book's main lessons into a series of automated emails that deliver value over time—each one gently reinforcing your authority and prompting readers to take the next step, whether that's booking a discovery call or attending a workshop.

4. Create Spin-Off Products and Services

A book often represents just the tip of your intellectual property. If your ideas resonate, readers will want more hands-on guidance from you. Consider developing spin-off offerings that provide a deeper, more personalized experience:

- Online Courses: Break your book into modules and turn it into a self-paced learning program. Add video lectures, worksheets, and assessments to help learners apply your frameworks.

- Interactive Workshops: Host live or virtual workshops where participants practice the tools and methods described in your book. These workshops can serve as introductory offers that lead to deeper consulting engagements.

- **Coaching Programs:** If your audience includes business owners, managers, or teams seeking direct support, consider offering short-term group coaching or one-on-one mentoring programs based on the teachings from your book.

These products don't just create additional revenue streams—they deepen your client relationships and extend the lifespan of your book's message.

Building A Thriving Ecosystem Around Your Book
1. Creating a Private Membership Community

As a consultant, your book's most significant impact isn't just in the ideas you share—it's in the conversations those ideas spark. A private membership community is one of the most effective ways to deepen reader engagement and establish yourself as a trusted resource.

Consider creating a group on platforms like Slack, Facebook Groups, Circle, or a dedicated membership site, where readers and clients can discuss the lessons from your book and apply them to their work. This space can evolve into a vibrant hub where:

- You host monthly Q&A sessions, clarifying your frameworks and helping readers implement them.

- Guest experts share complementary insights, adding value to your community.

- Members exchange real-world applications of your methods, fostering peer learning.

This type of community not only strengthens your relationship with your audience but also expands your influence beyond the book itself, turning passive readers into active participants in your consulting ecosystem.

2. Gathering and Showcasing Social Proof
a. Encouraging Reviews and Testimonials

Your book's credibility grows through reader feedback. While your initial launch may have gathered some early reviews, ongoing testimonials help your book appear fresh and relevant to new audiences. Every new review is a signpost of continued value.

Why Consultants Need Ongoing Reviews:

- They show that your ideas remain relevant in a changing business environment.

- New reviews can improve your book's visibility on Amazon and other platforms.

- Testimonials provide powerful marketing material for your consulting website, proposals, and social media.

Practical Strategies to Gather Reviews:

- Automated Email Follow-ups: If you offer a free chapter, workbook, or other lead magnet, follow up with readers 2-3 weeks later, inviting them to leave a review once they've applied your insights.

- Social Media Requests: Periodically post on LinkedIn or Twitter, reminding your audience that honest reviews help other professionals discover valuable resources.

- Review Circles: If you're connected to fellow consultant-authors, form a support circle where you ethically review each other's books and provide meaningful feedback.

b. Collecting Case Studies

Nothing showcases your expertise better than real-world results. Encourage your readers to share how your frameworks improved their businesses, leadership teams, or organizational processes.

- Written Testimonials: Ideal for landing pages, speaking proposals, and newsletters.

- Video Interviews: Conduct successful interviews with readers or clients via Zoom and post the recordings on LinkedIn, YouTube, and your website.

- Before-and-After Case Studies: Where applicable, highlight quantitative improvements, such as increased revenue, operational efficiencies, or leadership development outcomes.

3. Keeping Your Book Current With Updates or New Editions

As a consultant, your knowledge evolves, and your book should reflect that growth. A static book can quickly become outdated in fast-moving industries.

a. Why You Should Plan Updates:
- New insights and tools can replace the recommendations you originally made.

- Shifting business environments may require you to revise examples or add new frameworks.

- An updated edition provides an opportunity for renewed marketing and publicity.

b. Benefits of Revised Editions:
- Fresh Launch Moments: Treat a revised edition as a new release, complete with new media pitches, podcasts, and a social media push.

- Evergreen Accuracy: Keeping your ideas relevant prevents negative reviews and ensures the book continues adding value.

- Additional Revenue Opportunities: Consider launching a workbook, expanded edition, or companion guide to deepen reader engagement.

c. Bonus Materials to Consider:

- A bonus chapter exploring advanced strategies.

- An FAQs section addressing common reader questions.

- Expert interviews or roundtable discussions that extend your thought leadership.

4. Engaging With Your Reader Community Over Time
a. Host Live Sessions or AMAs (Ask Me Anything)

Long after your book's release, you can keep your audience engaged through virtual events such as:

- Live reading sessions where you unpack key chapters and share behind-the-scenes insights.

- Ask Me Anything (AMA) events, which allow readers and clients to ask questions about the challenges they're facing in applying your frameworks.

b. In-Person Meetups

If your consulting work involves travel or conferences, consider hosting casual meetups or book-signing sessions. These informal events strengthen your brand and turn readers into loyal advocates.

c. Regular Email Updates

If your book helped build your email list (through downloadable bonuses or chapter giveaways), continue nurturing that audience. Regular newsletters can share:

- New blog posts or articles expanding on your book's ideas.

- Announcements of upcoming workshops, webinars, or masterclasses.

- Readers' success stories and practical implementation tips.

Please keep the conversation going and subtly remind readers how your consulting services can help them take their goals further.

5. Monitoring Metrics and Adapting Over Time

To sustain your book's impact, keep an eye on the data:

a. Sales and Category Rankings

Observe patterns in your book sales. For example, do sales spike when you give a keynote, appear on a podcast, or launch a webinar series? Use these insights to focus on what works best for you.

b. Audience Demographics

Track your website, email list, and social media analytics. Are new industries showing interest? Are you unexpectedly popular in a particular country or region? Use these insights to explore translation opportunities, specialized webinars, or new service offerings.

c. Listening to Reader Feedback

Monitor your reviews, DMs, and emails for recurring themes. If multiple readers struggle with the same concept, consider creating a follow-up blog series or even a second book. If complaints arise, address them through clarifications within your community or updates to your content.

6. Sustaining Relevance as a Consultant-Author

Your consulting practice will evolve—your book should reflect that journey. Share openly how your latest experiences refine your original insights. This transparency keeps your audience engaged and shows that your frameworks aren't static; they're living, evolving, and battle-tested in the real world.

7. Creating a "Brand Orbit" Around Your Book

Your book should remain a central part of your brand. Reference it regularly:

- Include a link in your email signature.

- Mention it in podcast interviews or webinars.

- Revisit its lessons in your blog posts and LinkedIn articles.

Let it revolve around your other offerings, creating a cohesive narrative of who you are and what you stand for.

Action Plan for Sustained Momentum
- Map Out a Year of Micro-Promotions: Identify quarterly themes or industry events that align with your book's topic to create a targeted marketing strategy. Use these as hooks for fresh promotions.

- Host Post-Launch Events: Within 3 to 6 months, organize a book discussion session where readers can share feedback, ask questions, and discuss next steps with you.

- Develop a Repurposing Calendar: Break down each chapter into micro-content—blog posts, infographics, videos, and email series.

- Gather Social Proof: Proactively collect case studies and testimonials that showcase real-world success with your frameworks.

- Consider Future Products: At the 12- or 18-month mark, assess whether a second edition, workbook, or companion course is worthwhile to develop.

- Monitor What's Working: Keep tracking your key performance metrics to refine your post-launch strategy.

***

Next Steps

"Great consultants and great businesses have to be great storytellers, too. We have to tell stories – emotive, compelling stories – and even more so because we're nonfiction."

—**Angela Ahrendts**

Don't miss out on your chance to shine. Follow these steps for a clear understanding of how we can help you grow as a consultant thought leader.

Click the links below to kickstart your authorship journey:

https://stardombooks.com/clarity-session/

Step 1: This is a downloadable link on how to use your book as a consulting strategy.

Step 2: This is a community of other aspiring and growth-focused consultants that can be valuable for your journey.

Your success story starts here. Cheers to your future!

About the Author

RAAM ANAND
5-times Bestselling Author
Publishing Advisor to Top Leadership
Investor in Various Start-ups
Chief Editor & Publisher
High-performance Coach

Raam Anand coaches aspiring authors and non-writers to become published authors. He is a five-time international bestselling author and one of the most globally respected leadership coaches.

As the Chief Editor at Stardom Books (USA/India), Raam has published more than 260 authors while coaching people on productivity, personal branding, and book publishing. Official statistics and magazines report that Raam is one of the world's leading publishing coaches.

He has trained thousands of CXOs, experts, entrepreneurs, and thought leaders through his books, online courses, workshops, and conferences.

www.ingramcontent.com/pod-product-compliance
Lightning Source LLC
LaVergne TN
LVHW011422080426
835512LV00005B/213